Will You Help Me?

Also by Maggie Hartley

Will You Help Me?

RALPH'S TRUE STORY OF ABUSE,
SECRETS AND LIES

MAGGIE HARTLEY

WITH
HEATHER BISHOP

SEVEN DIALS

First published in Great Britain in 2024 by Seven Dials,
an imprint of The Orion Publishing Group Ltd
Carmelite House, 50 Victoria Embankment
London EC4Y 0DZ

An Hachette UK Company

1 3 5 7 9 10 8 6 4 2

ISBN (Mass Market Paperback) 978 1 3996 2092 5
ISBN (eBook) 978 1 3996 2093 2
ISBN (Audio) 978 1 3996 2094 9

Typeset by Born Group
Printed and bound in Great Britain by Clays Ltd, Elcograf S.p.A.

www.orionbooks.co.uk

Dedication

This book is dedicated to Ralph and Amena, and all the children who have passed through my home. It's been a privilege to have cared for you and to be able to share your stories. And to the children who live with me now: thank you for your determination, strength and joy and for sharing your lives with me.

Contents

A Message from Maggie

I wanted to write this book to give people an honest account of what it's like to be a foster carer, to talk about some of the challenges that I face on a day-to-day basis and some of the children that I've helped.

My main concern throughout all this is to protect the children who have been in my care. For this reason, all names and identifying details have been changed, including my own, and no locations have been included.

Being a foster carer is a privilege and I couldn't imagine doing anything else. My house is never quiet but I wouldn't have it any other way. I hope perhaps my stories inspire other people to consider fostering, as new carers are always desperately needed. In fact, the latest statistics are alarming. Ofsted figures from 2022 showed that the number of available homes for foster children in England had fallen by almost a quarter in four years. This comes at the same time as the number of children in the UK care system is at a record high. Foster carers are needed more than ever so please do look into it if it's something that you or someone you know has ever considered.

Maggie Hartley

ONE

Party Time

Today was supposed to be a happy day but the teenage girl in my arms was sobbing her heart out.

'I miss my m-mum,' sniffed Amena. 'I w-wish she was here.'

'I know you do, flower,' I soothed, stroking her long brown hair. 'I know you do.'

I'd been fostering Amena for the past eight months and today was her sixteenth birthday. Despite being as tall as me and looking so grown up, inside she was still a little girl who wanted her mummy.

Amena and her mum, Hodan, were originally from Somalia but they'd been in the UK for several years. Hodan's sister lived in France and when she'd been diagnosed with lung cancer at the beginning of the year, Hodan had gone over there to nurse her through surgery and treatment. With no other family in the UK and not wanting to take her daughter out of school, Hodan had sought help from Social Services and that's when Amena had come into my care.

She was such a lovely girl – polite, helpful, kind – and she had been easy to have around. Whatever other placements I had, she always adapted with ease to the other children and never once complained. Amena had seen her mum a couple of times, most recently three weeks ago. It had been the school summer holidays and Hodan had managed to get the money together to get a ferry back to the UK for a week. Amena had loved seeing her mum but understandably it had really unsettled her to have to say goodbye again.

It was just the two of them and I knew that they were incredibly close. This was the first birthday Amena had spent without her mother so I understood why she was feeling upset. All I could do was give her a hug and let her cry it out.

I'd tried my best to make the morning special for her. She'd just had a breakfast of pancakes and chocolate spread, and I'd wrapped lots of little gifts like make-up, stationery and toiletries and piled them up on the kitchen table. She'd been so pleased and excited, and now it was time for her to head off to school.

'I know you're sad not to see your mum today but you can give her a call later when you get home,' I told her.

She nodded and wiped the tears from her face.

'And remember you've got your party to look forward to tonight,' I added, affectionately tucking her hair behind her ear.

'I know,' she sniffed, giving me a weak smile. 'It'll be really cool.'

It was mid-September but the weather had been so warm and sunny that Amena had invited some girls round after school to have pizza and mocktails in the garden.

Amena was the only child that I was fostering at the minute so, once I'd waved her off to school, I was determined to have a productive day. Experience told me that that the peace and quiet was unlikely to last so I took the opportunity to catch up on some paperwork and life admin. Then after lunch, I started decorating the garden for Amena and her friends. I was keen to make it look lovely for her so I hooked some fairy lights up around the patio and tied some bunches of balloons onto the fence. I'd got some plastic glasses, paper umbrellas and cocktail stirrers for their mocktails and I prepared some bowls of crisps and other nibbles. I'd bought some pizzas for later on in the evening and a chocolate birthday cake.

By 2 p.m., everything was ready and I was just admiring my handiwork when my mobile rang. It was my supervising social worker from the fostering agency that I worked for.

'Hi, Becky,' I said. 'How are you?'

'I'm OK,' she replied. 'Is now a good time to talk? What are you up to?'

I explained about Amena's party.

'That sounds nice,' she said.

She hesitated.

'I'm sorry, this is probably not a great time for me to ask you this . . .'

Instinct told me exactly what she was going to say.

'Is it about a placement?' I asked her.

'I'm afraid it is,' she sighed. 'Social Services have just called me. They're desperately searching for a placement for a six-year-old boy.'

'OK,' I told her, sitting down at the kitchen table so I could concentrate.

3

Becky explained that his name was Ralph and he'd come into the care system three days ago although she didn't know the circumstances yet.

'Where's he been for the past three days then?' I asked curiously.

'Well, that's the thing,' said Becky. 'Apparently he's been through two foster carers already and they've both said they couldn't cope with him and asked Social Services to take him back.'

I was immediately intrigued. I could understand a teenager causing that much disruption but what on earth could a six-year-old do to make two people give notice on him so quickly?

'The social worker only dropped him off at the second carer's yesterday afternoon, and she called Social Services an hour ago to say that she'd decided not to carry on with the placement and that she wouldn't be picking him up from school this afternoon,' Becky explained.

'Do you know why?' I asked.

'I'm afraid not,' replied Becky.

She explained that his social worker was going to go and pick him up from school.

'I think they were hoping to find a carer by the end of the school day but obviously it's been tricky as many carers are wary when they hear he's already been moved twice,' she added.

'Poor little lad,' I sighed. 'Having all those moves will be really confusing for him.'

It was always upsetting to hear when children had been moved from carer to carer. I'd fostered some children who'd had multiple moves and it was always unsettling for them.

I knew what Becky was telling me would ring alarm bells with a lot of carers and put them off. However, I liked kids that were branded as 'difficult'. I enjoyed the challenge and finding out what made them tick. In fact, it was one of the reasons I'd gone into fostering in the first place. In my twenties, I'd got a job as a deputy matron at a residential boarding school for what were described at the time as 'maladjusted boys'. I lived on site and was on duty 24/7 during term time. It was intense and exhausting and it certainly wasn't easy, but I loved it. I liked stroppy kids and they seemed to respond well to me. When I eventually left there and started childminding, I missed the challenge.

'What do you reckon, Maggie?' asked Becky. 'Do you think you'd consider taking this little lad on?'

'I know it sounds silly but the only thing stopping me from saying yes is Amena's party,' I told her. 'She was so upset this morning about not being with her mum, and I don't want to have to call it off because I've got a new placement arriving.'

'Let me talk to the social worker and explain,' said Becky 'It might be that she was going to take him back to the office anyway so she could bring him to you later on tonight.'

I felt awful as I didn't want to keep a six-year-old hanging around.

'If they could bring him here around 7 p.m.,' I told her, 'the girls will probably all be going by then.'

It wasn't ideal but I wanted to make sure that, given his age, Ralph was fed, bathed and ready for bed by 8 or 9 p.m. otherwise it wasn't fair on him.

'Social Services are desperate to find a placement for him so I'm sure we can sort something out,' Becky told me.

'I'll wait to hear back from you then,' I said.

It was only when I put the phone down that I suddenly questioned what I had done. This little boy must have significant behavioural problems if two carers had given up on him so quickly, but in a way it made me even more determined to help him.

However, the clock was ticking. I knew Amena and her friends would be arriving at 3.45 p.m. so I would need to get everything ready for Ralph before they arrived.

I had two bedrooms that I used for fostering. Amena was in the smaller single one so Ralph could go into the bigger bedroom that had a bunk bed and a single bed in it. I'd just had it newly decorated as, after several placements, it had started to look a bit tatty and tired. I always liked to keep things neutral so the décor would work for either boys or girls. The walls were now a light grey colour and I'd had the cream curtains cleaned. I'd bought new blue and white striped duvets that I'd put on the beds. Everything looked a lot fresher in there now.

I had a set routine when a new placement was coming. I rooted around in my big storage cupboard for the essentials that Ralph would need tonight. I found some pyjamas that I'd picked up in the sales. They were for age seven but they'd do. I grabbed some fresh towels and a toothbrush and flannel. As he was coming from another carer, I hoped that they'd send on some clothes with him but I knew I had pants and socks and some jeans and a couple of T-shirts, so at least we could make do until we had a chance to go to the shops.

By 3.30 p.m., I was pretty much ready for both the party and Ralph's arrival. I could hear the girls chatting and laughing as Amena's key turned in the lock.

'Ahh, it's the birthday girl,' I smiled. 'How was your day?'

'Good,' she replied. 'They all sang "Happy Birthday" to me in tutor time, it was sooo embarrassing.'

Her friends giggled.

'I'm glad they made a fuss of you,' I laughed.

As they all trooped upstairs to Amena's room to get changed, I held her back.

'There's something I need to tell you, lovey,' I said in a low voice. 'I've got a new placement coming later on today.'

I didn't go into details but I explained that it was a six-year-old boy.

'He's with Social Services now and I didn't want it to be really late when he arrived,' I said. 'So I've asked if his social worker can bring him here around 7 p.m. I don't think it will affect your birthday gathering too much. I hope that's OK.'

Amena shrugged. 'Oh, that's so little,' she sighed. 'I bet he's really scared. No, I don't mind. We'll be out in the garden anyway.'

'Thanks for being so understanding, lovey,' I smiled. She was always so good-natured and adaptable.

I suddenly remembered Louisa was due to come over too to help with the party and see Amena on her birthday. I'd taken Louisa in as a teenager after both her parents had died in a car accident and she was in her twenties now. She worked as a nanny, was married to Charlie and they had a daughter called Edie who was nearly three. Although I'd never formally adopted Louisa, she was for all intents and purposes like my biological daughter and Edie called me 'Nana'.

I sent Louisa a quick message letting her know I was expecting a new placement so it was probably best not to call round.

I don't want to intimidate him by having lots of people in the house when he arrives, I typed. *He's only six.*

Completely understand. Let's catch up another time. Wish Amena a happy bday from us xx, she replied.

By the time the girls came downstairs in their jeans and tops, I'd put some music on and laid out all of the nibbles and the mocktail ingredients outside.

'Go and mix yourselves a drink, girls,' I smiled. 'There's some mocktail recipes on the table.'

'Thank you, Maggie,' smiled Amena. 'It looks lovely.'

To be honest, I didn't have an awful lot to do as the girls wanted to be left to their own devices. There was a lot of shrieking and laughing coming from the garden and thankfully they all seemed to be having a good time.

I kept checking my phone in case Becky had called me back. It wasn't until just before 5 p.m. that I finally heard from her.

'Sorry for the delay, Maggie,' she told me. 'I've been struggling to get hold of the social worker, Shelley. She's taken Ralph back to the office with her and she's going to bring him round to your house at 7 p.m. Is that OK?'

'That's fine by me,' I said. 'But won't the poor little mite be starving?'

'Shelley said not to worry, she will sort him out with something to eat,' replied Becky.

'That's really helpful of her,' I said.

'I think she was just relieved to have found a carer to take him,' Becky confessed.

'OK, well I'll be ready and waiting for 7 p.m.,' I told her.

'Send me a quick message to let me know that he got there safely if you get chance,' she said. 'Oh, and Maggie – good luck.'

'I've got a feeling I'm going to need it,' I replied.

And, as I put down the phone, I suddenly felt nervous about what the next few hours were going to bring and who this troubled little boy was who was on his way to my house.

TWO

Mayhem

By 6.45 p.m. most of Amena's friends had gone. There were just a couple of girls left who were waiting for one of their dads to pick them up.

I sat in the kitchen eating some pizza as I knew that as soon as Ralph arrived, it would be all systems go and I'd spend the rest of the evening getting him settled.

Amena came wandering in.

'Have you and your friends had enough to eat?' I asked her. 'There's loads of birthday cake left if you want another slice?'

'I'm fine, thanks,' she replied. 'What time is the little boy supposed to be coming?'

'Hopefully any minute now,' I said, glancing at my watch.

'My friends will be going soon,' she told me.

'Don't worry, flower,' I reassured her. 'Becky explained the situation to the social worker so she'll have to take us as she finds us.'

'We'll stay in the garden out of your way,' she said.

'Honestly you don't have to,' I told her. 'This is your home at the moment and it's your birthday – you don't have to hide away.'

I couldn't stop normal life from happening just because a new child was arriving.

After I'd finished my pizza, I looked at the clock. It was now just past 7 p.m. and there was still no sign of the social worker and Ralph, so I decided to start clearing up some of the party stuff. I was just rinsing some dishes in the sink when I heard a knock at the door.

At last, I thought. *This must be them.*

As I walked through to the hallway, I felt a flutter of anticipation about what I was about to face but also relief that the waiting was over and he was finally here.

I opened the front door, unsure of what to expect, to find a blonde woman in her thirties stood on the doorstep. She looked hot, sweaty and very harassed. Lurking behind her leg was a little boy.

He was pale and thin and had short brown hair that was unevenly cut as if someone had hacked at it with kitchen scissors. But it was his eyes that really caught my attention. They were a clear, pale blue colour and while most children who arrived at my doorstep initially tended to avoid eye contact, he stared up at me, unflinching.

'You must be Maggie,' said the woman. 'I'm Shelley, Ralph's social worker. Sorry we're a bit late. It took us a while to get in the car.'

She laughed nervously but she looked and sounded exhausted.

I crouched down so I was at Ralph's level.

'And you must be Ralph,' I smiled. 'I'm Maggie. I'm really pleased to meet you. Did Shelley explain that you're coming to stay at my house?'

Ralph stared at me but he didn't say a word. His gaze was so intense, it was almost unnerving.

'Do you want to come in and I can show you around?' I asked.

Suddenly he made a loud hacking noise in his throat and before I knew it, a huge globule of spit flew out of his mouth and hit me right in the eye.

'Ralph, no!' shouted Shelley.

Spit dripped down my cheek and by the time I'd instinctively wiped it off with the back of my hand, he'd run into the house.

'Maggie, I'm so sorry,' said Shelley apologetically, rummaging in her handbag and handing me a tissue.

'It's OK,' I told her. 'It's only spit. I'll survive.'

It certainly wasn't pleasant but it had happened to me before and I'm sure it would happen again.

There was so sign of Ralph and Shelley suddenly looked panicked.

'We'd better go and see what he's up to,' she gasped. 'He's what I'd call a very active child.'

I had no idea what she meant by that but I soon found out. As we walked into the house and through to the kitchen, the patio doors were wide open and I could hear the girls screaming outside.

'Yuck!' I heard one of them shriek. 'That's disgusting!'

Amena came running in.

'Maggie, the little kid is out there and he's doing a poo on the patio.'

'Oh no,' sighed Shelley, running outside.

'It's OK, lovey, we'll sort it,' I told Amena.

As I dashed outside, I could see that Ralph had pulled down his pants and the grey tracksuit bottoms that he was wearing and was squatting down next to the mocktail table, making loud straining noises. Amena's two friends, Lottie and Chloe, were shrieking in horror.

'Eurgh,' Chloe squealed. 'It stinks.'

Shelley looked mortified and clearly didn't know what to do.

'I'm so sorry, Maggie,' she sighed. 'He did this at Social Services earlier.'

'Honestly, it's OK,' I said.

I went over to Ralph who had finished relieving himself on my flagstones.

'Ralph, we don't do poos and wees outside,' I said calmly. 'We do them in the toilet. Come inside with me and I'll get you cleaned up.'

He stared at me.

'No!' he shouted. Suddenly he started making the same hacking noise. This time I knew what was coming and I managed to duck out of the way as a globule of phlegm came flying past me and landed on the table.

'Eurgghh, that's gross!' shrieked Lottie.

I could see Amena was mortified.

'Why don't you take your friends to the front room and watch a bit of telly and I'll clean up out here?' I suggested.

'OK,' she said and the three of them fled inside.

Before I had the chance to grab him, Ralph was on the move again. He was shuffling around the garden still with his pants and tracksuit bottoms around his ankles and had started making a loud whooping noise.

'Ralph, come back here now,' shouted Shelley firmly. 'You need to get cleaned up.'

He ignored her and carried on running around in circles.

'Whoop! Whoop! Whoop!' he yelled.

'Ralph!' she shouted. 'You're going to fall.'

The more Shelley called him, the faster Ralph ran and the louder he whooped.

He ripped the balloons down from the fence and pulled down the fairy lights, then he shuffled over to the flower bed and started pulling up all of my plants and throwing them across the grass.

'Ralph!' shouted Shelley. 'That's enough, you're ruining Maggie's garden!'

She turned to me and asked, 'Shall I try and catch him?'

'It's OK,' I told her calmly. 'I think it will wind him up even more if we start chasing him. He's safe out here. He can't get out or hurt himself on anything so let's just leave him and go inside. I bet he'll soon lose interest.'

'But what about your lovely flowers?' asked Shelley.

'Oh, they're the least of my worries,' I smiled. 'I can always plant more.'

My thinking was that if we moved inside and Ralph couldn't see us, that would automatically bring him in.

Sure enough, a few minutes later, he came stumbling through the patio doors.

'Whoop, whoop!' he yelled.

But before we could stop him, he'd shuffled through to the hallway and into the living room where the girls were watching TV. They started screaming as he did a lap of the room still with his trousers and pants around his ankles.

'Yuck, I can see his willy!' laughed Chloe.

Enough was enough.

I knew I needed to come up with a plan to put a stop to this chaos. Ralph needed to be cleaned up and get his clothes back on.

'OK, let's try and lure him back to the kitchen,' I told Shelley. 'Then I can try to get him in a caring cuddle.'

It was something that I'd been taught on a training course where you put your hands around a child in a C-shape so you were making a ring around them. There were lot of rules and regulations around restraining children and there were techniques that we were taught in our training to do it safely and carefully. A caring cuddle was firm yet gentle and didn't cause any distress. It was a good one to use when a child was out of control or in danger of hurting themselves or someone else. It was less threatening for them not to have eye contact with you and they would still be able to see everything happening around them.

We walked through to the kitchen in the hope that Ralph would follow. I spotted a fleecy blanket, which I grabbed and passed to Shelley.

'Please could you hold that for now and give it to me once I've got him?' I asked her.

She nodded although she looked confused.

'He's got poo all over him so I'm going to wrap him in that,' I told her.

'Good idea,' she nodded.

I closed and locked the patio doors so if Ralph did appear, there was no chance of him escaping outside again. A few seconds later, he suddenly ran through the door and into the kitchen.

'Whoop, whoop, whoop!' he yelled.

This time I was ready for him. I managed to get behind him and put my arms around him in a C shape.

'Blanket, please,' I said to Shelley.

As soon as she passed it to me, I wrapped it around Ralph's body like I was swaddling a baby. Then I gently and carefully sank to the floor with him so he ended up sat on my lap with my arms around him.

Ralph looked surprised but thankfully he didn't struggle.

'There you go,' I told him gently. 'You must be exhausted after all of that running around.'

'Whoop! Whoop! Whoop!' he yelled.

There was no way I was letting Ralph go again so I chatted to Shelley while I held him on my lap on the kitchen floor.

'How do you want to play this, Maggie?' she asked me.

I knew we probably had limited time for Ralph to be still.

'I think my main priority is to get him cleaned up,' I told her. 'And I think the best way to do that is by giving him a bath.'

'You must be getting tired, Ralph,' I said, looking down at him. 'We need to start thinking about getting you to bed.'

'Whoop!' he yelled and I could feel him beginning to struggle.

'I know we haven't had chance to chat but is it OK if we do that tomorrow?' I asked Shelley.

'Absolutely,' she nodded, obviously relieved. 'I'll leave you to get settled and I can ring you first thing in the morning.'

'If there's anything urgent that you think I really need to know tonight then please call me,' I told her. 'And what should I do about school?'

'Let's not worry about school for now,' she replied.

I still knew nothing at all about Ralph. Ideally I would have liked to know why he'd come into the care system and also why he'd been through so many carers in such a small space of time, although seeing how he'd behaved since arriving at my house told me pretty much all I needed to know.

'Let's go and say bye-bye to Shelley now,' I told him.

'Whoop!' he replied.

There was no way I was letting him out of my grip, so I made sure the blanket was safely tucked around his shoulders so he wouldn't trip then I held firmly onto his hand and led him out to the hallway.

'Please call me if you need anything,' Shelley told me and I nodded.

'Let's catch up in the morning,' I replied.

Once she'd gone, still keeping a firm hold of Ralph's hand, I poked my head around the living room door and explained to Amena what was happening.

'I'll be upstairs with Ralph if you need me,' I told her and she nodded.

'And bye, girls,' I added to Lottie and Chloe, who looked bemused after the mayhem that had just unfolded in front of them.

As I led Ralph slowly and carefully up the stairs, thankfully he was quiet. We walked into the bathroom and I sat on the floor and put him down on my lap again with my arms around him.

'I know it must be scary for you, coming to stay at another new house,' I said to him. 'But I promise I'll look after you.'

I talked him through everything I was going to do.

'In a minute I'm going to stand up and run you a nice bath. I'll turn the taps on and water will fill the bath and I'm going to put some bubble bath in there so it's all bubbly,' I explained.

'Then I'm going to get a flannel and make sure you're nice and clean. Then we'll get you into some clean PJs and we can go and have a look at your bedroom where you'll be sleeping tonight.'

He'd been very still and quiet but if I was going to run him a bath, I knew I was going to have to let him get off my lap. Carefully I lifted him off me and onto the floor. But as soon as I stood up, Ralph jumped up too and started running in circles around the bathroom.

By the time I'd turned my back to him to put the plug in the bath and turn on the taps, he'd thrown mine and Amena's toothbrushes down the loo.

'Whoop! Whoop!' he yelled, grabbing the toothpaste and squeezing it all over the floor.

While I squirted some bubble bath in, he sprayed Amena's deodorant and threw the can at the wall. Then he ran over to the airing cupboard and started pulling out all of the towels.

'No, Ralph,' I told him sternly. 'We don't do that with the towels.'

I took deep breaths and tried to stay calm despite the carnage Ralph was unleashing around me. I knew it could all be cleaned up later; I just needed to focus on the task in hand and get him into the bath.

Eventually I managed to swaddle him in the blanket again and we sat back down on the floor.

'Right, we're going to have a bath now,' I told him firmly. 'We need to get you nice and clean.'

With him still sitting on my lap, I quickly managed to get his clothes off then I lifted him into the water.

At first, he refused to sit down and started kicking the bubbles.

'Ralph, I need you to sit down please,' I said. 'Otherwise you're going to fall.'

'Whoop, whoop!' he shouted, splashing some water at me.

I put my hands under his armpits and lifted him up and thankfully this time his legs bent and he sat in the bath. He started bashing his hand down on the surface of the water. Bubbles and water splashed everywhere and the bathroom floor was soaked.

'Let's see if we can keep the water in the bath,' I smiled.

But then, after a few seconds, he suddenly went quiet and I could see that, thankfully, he was starting to relax. Baths always seemed to have the desired effect. They were a good way to calm children down and soothe them – and also to contain them.

I tried to make washing Ralph into a bit of a game.

'Oh no, it's raining,' I said as I squeezed the sponge over his back and he gave me a shy smile.

As I gently washed him down, I talked to him to try to distract him.

'I know it must feel strange coming to another new house,' I soothed. 'But you're going to sleep here now and we'll make sure that you're nice and comfy.

'What sort of toys do you like playing with?' I asked him. 'Are there any special foods that you like to eat?'

Ralph stared up at me with those piercing blue eyes but didn't say a word. Shelley had told me that he wasn't very verbal and I wondered what on earth he must be thinking.

Although he was calm right now, I wasn't sure how long it was going to last so I didn't want him to spend too much time in the bath.

After I'd gently washed him down, I lifted him out of the water and wrapped a clean towel around him.

'All done,' I smiled.

I made a mental note to put the blanket straight in the wash as it'd had Ralph's bare bottom against it.

'I've got some lovely pyjamas all ready for you,' I told him. 'They've got dogs on them. Do you like doggies, Ralph?'

He stared at me.

'Sausages!' he yelled suddenly.

I was confused by his response but then I realised that he was answering the question that I'd asked him a moment ago.

'Oh, so sausages are your favourite food, are they?' I asked him and he nodded.

'They're my favourite too,' I smiled. 'I like to have mine with mashed potatoes and beans.'

'I like sausages,' he replied.

It was the first coherent sentence that he'd said to me and it felt like progress. Despite the absolute chaos that he'd caused since he'd arrived, I was hopeful that he'd stay calm and I could finally get him settled for the night.

THREE

The Longest Night

The bath thankfully seemed to have done the trick and Ralph was much calmer. However, I wasn't prepared to take any chances and I gripped his hand as I led him to his bedroom.

'This is where you're going to sleep,' I told him, showing him the single bed.

'I know there are three beds but it's only going to be you staying in here,' I reassured him, just in case he thought there might be other children sleeping in the bunk beds.

I could see him looking around the room curiously. I was all too aware that this was the third strange house that he'd been to in as many days and I knew it must be so confusing for him.

'Shall we go downstairs and get you a drink?' I asked him and he nodded.

I was also keen to check on Amena. I'd heard the front door open and close when I was giving Ralph a bath so I assumed that Lottie and Chloe had been picked up by now.

She was in the living room watching TV. She looked suspiciously at Ralph, who was standing quietly at my side.

'Are you OK, flower?' I asked her.

'Yep,' she replied. 'I've just spoken to Mum. She gave me a call to wish me happy birthday.'

I noticed that her eyes were all red and puffy and I could tell that she'd been crying.

'I'm glad that she managed to get hold of you,' I smiled. 'I bet she's sad not to be with you on your special day.'

'She is,' shrugged Amena. 'But I know Aunty needs her more.'

Ralph had been standing there holding my hand.

'Cars,' he said suddenly. 'I like cars.'

Amena stared at him, puzzled, but I suddenly realised what he was talking about.

'I think Ralph's answering a question that I asked him earlier about what toys he likes,' I smiled.

'I like cars,' he repeated.

'It's good that you've come to Maggie's house then,' Amena told him. 'She's got lots of cars in her toy cupboard.'

'Amena's right,' I told him. 'How about we go into the kitchen and you can choose a car that you might want to take up to your bedroom with you?'

Ralph didn't say anything but his eyes were wide as I opened the toy cupboard and brought out a big plastic box filled with all sorts of cars.

'You choose one while I get you a drink,' I encouraged him.

While I warmed up some milk, Ralph stared at the toy cars for ages, then tentatively reached his arm in and grabbed a red dumper truck. I handed him his milk and watched him glug it down while he sat on the floor next to the truck. I was a firm believer in the magical power of warm milk. Like a bath, it helped to soothe a child and calm them down.

Ralph suddenly seemed like a different child to the one who had arrived on my doorstep earlier. Perhaps he'd spent the day kicking off and was now exhausted? Or maybe his behaviour wasn't as out of control as I had assumed? Whatever the reason, I wasn't going to question it.

After he'd finished his milk, I led him back upstairs.

'I'm going to take you to the toilet now,' I told him.

After what had happened earlier in the garden, I wasn't taking any chances. Even though he was six, I wasn't sure if he was toilet trained and I was prepared to put him in a pull-up overnight if he needed it.

The bathroom was still a mess from Ralph's earlier escapades. Before he used the loo, I put on some rubber gloves and fished mine and Amena's toothbrushes out of the toilet bowl and put them straight in the bin.

'I'd like you to try and do a wee for me before bed, please,' I told him.

I lifted up the toilet seat and as he pulled down his pyjamas, I quickly left the bathroom. He clearly knew what to do.

When I heard him coming out, I encouraged him to wash his hands then I gave him a toothbrush and helped him brush his teeth. He looked a bit bewildered but he went along with what I was doing, then I took him into his bedroom.

'It's night-night time now, Ralph,' I told him.

I pulled back the duvet and he climbed into bed.

It struck me again how little I knew about this boy. I didn't know anything about his birth parents, how he'd been treated or why he'd been brought into care. I'd met his most basic of needs and that's all I could do tonight. I knew that most young children liked predictability, structure and routine and they liked to know what was going to happen. So I talked to Ralph about the following day in the hope that it would bring him some comfort.

'Tomorrow when you wake up, we'll go downstairs and sit at the table and have breakfast,' I told him. 'What shall we have for our breakfast?'

Ralph was silent for a moment.

'I like sausages,' he said.

'I know you like sausages,' I told him. 'But I'm afraid I don't have any in my fridge at the moment. But I promise you that tomorrow we'll go out to the shops to get some and we'll have them for tea tomorrow night.

'What about cereal or toast?' I asked. 'Do you like them?'

'Toast,' he nodded.

'Well, I shall make sure that I have a big plate of toast all ready for you and I've got some butter and jam too.'

He stared up at me with those piercing eyes. I noticed he was still clutching the dumper truck.

'Do you want me to put your truck on the bedside table before you go to sleep?' I asked him.

'No,' he said firmly, clasping it tightly in his fist.

I tucked the duvet in around him.

'Night night, Ralph and dumper truck,' I told him. 'Sleep well and I'll see you in the morning.'

I turned the lamp off and left the bedroom door ajar so there was a little bit of light coming in from the landing. Ralph didn't say a word as I left the room.

That was easier than expected, I thought to myself.

I went back into the bathroom and finished tidying up the mess from earlier. I folded up the towels and put them back in the airing cupboard, replaced mine and Amena's tooth-brushes and wiped the toothpaste off the floor. By the time I'd finished, it was still all quiet from Ralph's room. I didn't want to check on him too soon and potentially disturb him so I headed downstairs.

Before I sat down with Amena, I knew I needed to give my fostering agency a quick ring. My supervising social worker, Becky, wasn't on call tonight but I was able to speak to the duty worker, Liz.

I confirmed that Ralph had arrived and explained that I'd had to swaddle him and hold him on my lap for his own safety. If you ever had to restrain a child, you always had to log it for safeguarding reasons.

'He was absolutely feral when he arrived,' I told Liz. 'Wrapping him in the blanket was the best option as it stopped him from getting poo everywhere and also gave him a bit of dignity.'

'It sounds like you did absolutely the right thing,' she said.

'Thankfully he calmed down a lot after I gave him a bath,' I told her.

She logged everything onto the system and said that Becky would be in touch in the morning.

Once I'd finished the call, I went into the living room to see Amena, making sure to leave the door open so I could hear any potential noise coming from upstairs.

'Ralph's in bed,' I announced, sinking down on the sofa.

'He was crazy when he first came,' she sighed. 'I can't believe he did a poo on the patio.'

'I know,' I replied. 'Poor thing was probably feeling very anxious about coming to a new place.'

27

'He's only little,' she nodded. 'He must have been really scared. At least I'm old enough to understand why I had to come here. Where are his mum and dad?'

'I honestly don't know, lovey,' I told her. 'With all the commotion, I just needed to try and calm him down, get him in the bath and to bed, so I didn't have time to chat much to his social worker. Hopefully I'll find out more tomorrow.'

However, even if I did find out, I knew I wouldn't be able to share it with Amena for confidentiality reasons.

We watched TV together for a bit and had a slice of birthday cake. All the while, I had one ear out listening for any noise coming from upstairs. But all was quiet and it seemed as if Ralph had settled.

At 10 p.m., Amena went up to bed.

'Night-night, flower,' I told her. 'I hope you've had a good birthday.'

'It was really good, thanks,' she smiled.

I was pretty shattered myself so I decided to head to bed as well. But I wanted to check on Ralph first.

I held my breath as I pushed the door open as quietly as I could. As I peered in, I could see that he was lying on his side facing the wall. Even though I couldn't see his face, he was quiet and it looked like he was asleep.

I got into bed and lay there in the dark, thinking about Ralph. I was pleased that I'd eventually got a couple of sentences out of him and I knew that he was capable of listening and being calm. But I was still scarred by the way he'd behaved in the first hour with me. Was that what he was going to be like every day or was he just fuelled by anxiety about being moved to yet another carer?

*

It was after midnight and I must have been about to nod off when a noise suddenly jolted me back awake.

An almighty bang ricocheted across the landing.

Crash. Thud.

I leapt up out of bed and ran down the landing to Ralph's room where I instinctively knew the noise was coming from. The light was off but I could see that the room was in disarray.

Somehow he'd managed to pull the curtains down. The rail had come out of the wall and the chest of drawers had been pushed over. Ralph was wide awake and jumping up and down on his bed.

'What on earth are you doing?' I asked him as I turned on the light.

'Whoop! Whoop!' he yelled.

He had the dumper truck in his hand and he banged it hard against the wall several times so it made holes in the plaster.

'No, Ralph,' I told him. 'We don't bang the wall like that.'

I walked towards him but as I tried to take the dumper truck, he raised his hand and slammed it into my face. I stumbled back in shock as a sharp pain seared across my cheek.

'Maggie?' said a voice suddenly. 'What's happening?'

Amena was standing in the doorway in her pyjamas.

'Sorry, lovey, Ralph's a bit unsettled so I'm just trying to calm him down,' I told her. 'You try and go back to sleep.'

'It's so noisy,' she sighed groggily.

'I know,' I said. 'Hopefully I can settle him back down soon.'

But Ralph was showing no signs of calming down. He was standing on the bed flicking the bedside light on and off.

The room looked like a whirlwind had hit it but most of it could wait until morning. I knew that somehow I needed to get Ralph back into bed.

'Ralph, it's night-night time now,' I told him firmly.

I took him by the hand but he shook me off and started jumping up and down on the bed.

'Whoop, whoop, whoop!' he yelled.

'Ralph, it's bedtime now,' I repeated but he ignored me.

He jumped onto the floor and started running around the bedroom. Meanwhile, I got a travel blind out of the wardrobe and stuck it over the window as a temporary fix until I could sort out the curtains in the morning.

I managed to get hold of Ralph's hand and I led him over to the bed.

'It's night-time now, Ralph,' I told him. 'I need you to get into bed please.'

He got into bed but he didn't lie down.

I went and turned the light off to see if the darkness helped to settle him. Then I sat down on the bed next to him.

'I'm going to sit here, Ralph, until you lie down and go to sleep.'

'No!' he said.

Before I could grab him, he leapt out of bed and started pulling books out of a little bookcase I had in the corner of the room and throwing them across the floor. I knew I couldn't keep trying to catch him and lead him back to bed. All I could do was sit there and hope that eventually he would lose interest and get bored or tired.

'I'm not going anywhere, Ralph, until you get back into bed and go to sleep,' I told him.

In my experience, children could only have a meltdown for so long before they wore themselves out. I would only intervene if he was in danger of hurting himself.

I sat there in the darkness while Ralph opened and closed the wardrobe door and pulled some bedding out of one of the drawers. Then he sat on the floor and threw some books around.

'Whoop!' he yelled.

I was utterly exhausted and I was sure he must be too. Eventually, about an hour later, I held my breath as he came back over to the bed and lay down. He curled up on top of the duvet like a cat.

I didn't dare move him or put him under the covers and I wanted to stay there with him until I was sure he was 100 per cent asleep and settled. As I heard his breathing deepen, I lowered myself off the bed and, very slowly, edged my way across the floor to the door.

I had one last look across the room. In the darkness, I could see his chest rise and fall and hear him sigh.

At last he was asleep.

I crept back across the landing to my room. As I collapsed onto my bed, I looked at the clock.

It was 2.30 a.m.

It had been over two hours of hell trying to get him back to sleep. My cheek stung from where he'd lashed out at me but I hadn't had the chance to look in the mirror yet. To be honest, I was exhausted. As soon as my head hit the pillow, my eyes closed and I drifted off into a deep sleep.

FOUR

Morning Has Broken

It felt like I'd only been asleep for a few minutes when I woke up with a start. There were bangs and crashes and what sounded like glass smashing.

Ralph.

It was followed by yelling.

'Stop it! Get off my stuff!'

I suddenly realised it was Amena's voice. In an absolute panic, I ran down the landing to her bedroom. Amena was sat up in bed, a horrified look on her face, while Ralph was stood by her dressing table throwing things on the floor. Her make-up was all over the carpet and he'd smashed a bottle of perfume.

'Maggie, he's ruining my stuff and he smells disgusting,' she sighed.

'I'm so sorry, lovey,' I said in a quiet voice.

To be honest, the overpowering smell of perfume was very welcome as, when I took a closer look at Ralph, I saw that his pyjama bottoms were covered in poo.

My heart sank.

'Whoop! Whoop!' he yelled, grabbing Amena's pens from her pencil case and hurling them across the room.

'Please make him stop,' she pleaded. 'He's already drawn on the walls.'

She was right. On the wall behind her desk were big scribbles of black marker.

'Ralph, you need to stop this,' I told him firmly. 'These are not your things.'

He ignored me and picked up Amena's jewellery box and tipped out all of the contents onto the floor.

I could see that I was going to have to physically make him stop. But there was no way I was going to try to pick Ralph up in the state that he was in. So I darted out of the room, quickly grabbed a towel off the banister and wrapped it around him. He wriggled around in my arms but I managed to hang onto him.

'No, Ralph, we're going to go to the bathroom now,' I told him firmly. 'We need to get you cleaned up.'

I gave Amena a pleading look that said I'm really sorry.

'I'll help you tidy this up later, flower,' I told her as I ushered him out of her bedroom and along the landing.

The clock in the bathroom told me that it was only 6.30 a.m. Ralph had been asleep for the grand total of four hours and it was no wonder I felt like a zombie.

My head spun with tiredness and I suddenly realised that my cheek was throbbing. When I caught sight of myself in the bathroom mirror, I saw there was a big red mark on my face where I remembered Ralph had whacked me with the dumper truck last night. But there was no time to think about it. I had my arm around him but he was struggling to break free. I didn't want him running around the house covered in poo again, so I knew I needed to act quickly. Normally I'd run him a bath, but this was about getting Ralph clean as soon as possible rather than just soothing him so I decided to give him a shower. Using one hand, I managed to put the shower on and check the temperature while firmly keeping an arm around Ralph with the other. Then I quickly got his pyjamas off and lifted him into the shower cubicle.

'You're going to have a lovely warm shower and get nice and clean,' I told him.

But as soon as the water hit Ralph's head, he started to scream.

'No, no, no!' he yelled, bolting out of the cubicle.

He cowered in the corner of the bathroom, naked and shivering.

'Ralph, what's the matter?' I asked, walking over and crouching down so I was close to him. 'We really need to get you clean.'

'No,' he whimpered and I could see he was shaking in fear.

'What is it?' I asked him gently. 'Don't you like the shower?'

He shook his head. I knew some children didn't like the feeling of the water on their face.

'You don't have to have the water on your head if you don't want to,' I told him. 'Look, come over here and I'll show you.'

He followed me nervously back to the cubicle where I unhooked the shower head and turned the water on.

'See,' I smiled. 'You can hold it and put the water where you want it. It doesn't have to go on your face or your head. If you get back in then I can show you.'

Ralph stepped hesitantly into the shower cubicle. He still looked terrified but I gently sprayed his toes and then I handed the showerhead to him.

I tried to make a game out of it.

'Can you spray your legs?' I asked him.

He nodded and did as I asked.

'Well done,' I smiled. 'Now can you spray your arms? Good boy.'

We worked our way all around his body, everywhere except his head and his face, and while he was doing that, I managed to quickly wash him down with a sponge and some shower gel.

'There you go,' I told him. 'That wasn't so bad was it? You're all clean and fresh again now.'

I helped him to dry himself while I put his soiled pyjamas into a plastic bag. I realised I was going to have to get some clean clothes for him from his bedroom. He'd only arrived with what he was wearing and those clothes were soiled and soaking downstairs. Last night I'd got a few things out of my cupboard that were age six but they were in his bedroom.

Ralph thankfully seemed a bit calmer after his shower but I knew I needed to try to keep him occupied so he didn't go running back to Amena's room and cause more chaos. I got a boxful of bath toys out.

'Wow, Ralph, look at these,' I said.

He immediately came running over, sat down on the floor and started to look through them.

'I'm just going to get you some clothes,' I told him. 'I'll be back in two minutes.'

I hadn't been into his bedroom yet this morning and, given the state of his pyjamas, I was dreading what I was going to find. As I pushed open the door, it was the smell that hit me first. It was so overpowering, it made me retch.

He'd pooed right in the middle of the room on the carpet but with dismay I realised that he'd managed to get it everywhere. There were handprints of poo up the walls, all over the chest of drawers, on the bookcase and even on the back of the door. There were smears of poo on the curtains that were still lying on the floor from where he'd pulled them down last night and on the wardrobes, as well as on the bedding on the bunk beds. I couldn't believe how far he'd managed to spread it.

I felt like crying. I didn't know where to start and also when I was going to have the time to clean it all up.

I knew it wasn't Ralph's fault and there were many reasons why children did this. It could be anger, anxiety or boredom, or a lot of the time it was the simple fact that no one had shown them how to use the toilet or they had been allowed to go to the toilet on the floor at home so it was seen as normal. I didn't know Ralph well enough yet to know which of those it was.

I wasn't angry at him – it was just overwhelming. But I knew there was nothing I could do now.

Breathing through my mouth, I quickly grabbed some clothes for him from the wardrobe and headed back to the bathroom.

Much to my amazement, he was still sitting calmly on the floor, playing with the bath toys.

'I'm going to get you dressed now but first I'd like you to try and have a wee,' I told him.

Like the night before, he seemed to know what to do when I took him to the toilet. So while he did a wee, I tidied up the bath toys.

I went over to him after he'd finished but I noticed that he hadn't flushed it. Funnily enough, I remembered he'd done the same thing the night before.

'When you've done a wee, you flush the toilet and then you wash your hands,' I told him gently. 'Just like this.'

But as I reached for the flush, Ralph let out the most horrendous scream.

'No!' he yelped.

He started running around in circles.

'Whoop! Whoop! Whoop!' he chanted, with his fingers in his ears.

The more time I spent with Ralph, the more I realised that the whooping was happening when he was feeling anxious.

'That's the noise the toilet makes when it flushes,' I explained. 'It's just the water washing your wee away so it's nice and clean for the next person. It's not going to hurt you. Come over here and I'll show you.'

'No,' he said firmly, picking up a toilet roll and hurling it at my head.

I could see he was out of control again. He ran over to the sink and swept everything off the shelf above it, then started throwing tubs of moisturiser and bottles of toiletries into the bath.

'Ralph, please stop this,' I urged.

It felt like he was slowly trashing my house, room by room.

When he started kicking the bathroom wall, I knew I needed to calm him down quickly as he was going to hurt himself. He was still naked apart from the bath towel wrapped around him and I knew that somehow I needed to get him dressed.

So I tried a technique that I'd used quite a lot in the past. It wasn't anything that I'd been taught but more something I did instinctively with children that had developed over time. I went over to Ralph and put my hands on either side of his face. It was enough to make him stop in his tracks.

'Look at my nose, Ralph,' I told him calmly. 'Look at my nose.'

He was so puzzled, or perhaps surprised, that he did exactly what I'd asked him to. His piercing blue eyes stared into mine.

'Good boy,' I said. 'We need to get you dressed now.'

'Look at my nose!' he repeated, parroting me, and we both ended up giggling.

After everything that had happened since he'd arrived, it was so lovely to hear Ralph giggle.

I think the technique worked because it was a sensory thing. Young children especially are soothed by touch and if they're looking at your nose then they're automatically making eye contact with you. Somehow it acted as a bit of a reset.

However, it had only calmed Ralph down to a certain degree. To get him dressed, I still had to sit on the floor with him wedged firmly between my knees to stop him from running off. It was a struggle but I managed to wrestle his arms into a T-shirt and quickly pull on some pants and shorts. By the time we headed downstairs, I was exhausted and it wasn't even 7.30 a.m. yet.

Amena came down shortly afterwards dressed in her school uniform. I went over and had a quiet word with her.

'I'm so sorry about your room, flower,' I told her. 'I'll go and sort out the mess when you're at school.'

'It's OK, I've done most of it,' she told me. 'But my carpet's a bit of a mess.'

39

'I'll replace all of the make-up and anything else he smashed,' I added.

'I can't believe he did that,' she sighed and I could see she was upset. 'Is he always going to be like that, pooing everywhere and destroying my stuff?'

'Hopefully not,' I told her. 'He's probably feeling very unsettled and scared – I'm sure things will settle down.'

I really hoped so. It was hard dealing with Ralph's behaviour but to see Amena upset too was just soul-destroying.

Once breakfast was out of the way and Amena had left for school, I knew I would have to tackle Ralph's bedroom. I felt sick at the state of it but it had to be done. However, I would have to occupy Ralph in a way which meant he wouldn't do any more damage. I knew he liked cars so I got the big box of them from the kitchen and took them upstairs. I shut all of the doors to the other rooms, put the cars on the landing and sat down with Ralph on the carpet.

'Look at all these lovely cars,' I told him. 'I thought you might like to play with them while I tidy up your room.'

He didn't say anything but he didn't need to, I could see he was already transfixed. I sat with him while he took each car out and had a good look at it, and then lined them all up on the carpet.

'Yellow car, red truck, black car, racing car,' he chanted.

'Ooh, this is a lovely one,' I said, picking up a blue bin truck. Ralph looked up at me, horrified.

'No! No!' he yelled, snatching it off me and lining it up again.

I could see that he was in his own little world and I felt that he was in a calm enough space that I could go into his bedroom and try to tackle the mess. The first thing I did was open the window to let some fresh air in to help with the smell. While trying not to gag, I put a nappy sack over my hand, picked up the poo and put it outside in the bin. Then I sprayed and scrubbed the carpet with cleaner. I stripped Ralph's bed and the bunk beds down to the waterproof mattress covers and put all of the bedding in the bath to soak.

Next I got a bucket, filled it with hot water and disinfectant and started washing everything down from the walls to the furniture. I kept one eye on Ralph, who was still playing happily with the cars on the landing.

I put the curtains in a bin bag so I could take them to a laundrette as they were too bulky to go in my machine. I decided to leave the travel blind up as at least that was waterproof and a wipeable material. After nearly an hour of scrubbing and washing, everything looked much better and smelt a lot fresher.

All I could hope was that that was the end of Ralph's destructive behaviour. It had to be, otherwise I wasn't sure that I could cope and inside of me a voice was questioning – what had I done? Had I made the right decision in taking on this little boy or had I made a terrible mistake?

FIVE

Supermarket Sweep

By 9 a.m. I was already so exhausted, I felt like having a nap. I'd just finished cleaning Ralph's bedroom when the phone rang.

It was Shelley, his social worker.

'Hi, Maggie, how are things?' she asked.

I took a deep breath, not knowing where to start.

'You could say it's been an eventful twelve hours,' I said.

'Oh no,' she laughed nervously, clearly worried I was about to give notice on him like the other two carers had. 'But Ralph's OK?'

'He's fine,' I replied. 'He's just playing with some toy cars.'

'Oh great,' she said, sounding relieved.

'I know we said we'd catch up this morning but I realised I've got a couple of meetings. So is it OK if I pop round to see you this afternoon?'

'Yes, of course,' I told her.

With Shelley not coming until later, I knew we had to quickly nip out to the supermarket. I needed to get some clothes for Ralph and I hadn't forgotten that I'd promised him sausages for tea.

'We're going to go to the shop now,' I told him. 'We need to get some sausages as I know they're your favourite.'

'No,' he told me, shaking his head. 'No, no, no!'

Having witnessed how out of control and destructive he could be, I was anxious about taking him in the car. I had no idea if he was used to going in cars but I remembered how dishevelled and stressed Shelley had been when she'd arrived with him last night so I was prepared for the fact that I was probably going to have a battle on my hands.

I decided to put him in a car seat with a five-point harness, which I knew would be more secure and harder for him to take off than one that used a regular seatbelt. As I lifted him into it, I gave him a couple of cars to hold – one in each hand.

'Look at that red racing car,' I told him. 'And the jeep is really cool, isn't it? I'd love to go for a drive in a jeep.'

They were the perfect distraction while I strapped him in.

So far, so good, I thought to myself.

Thankfully the supermarket was only ten minutes away and during the drive, I chatted to him. I talked about the big shop we were going to and how it sold lots of things, and that we were going to get some clothes for him to wear and some pyjamas and pants.

'Then you can choose the sausages and decide how many we're all going to have,' I told him. 'I think I can only eat two but you and Amena might want three or even four each if you're really hungry. Do you think you could eat four sausages?' I asked.

Ralph didn't say anything but thankfully he was quiet as he carefully examined the cars he was still clinging onto.

'Here we are,' I said, pulling up into the car park.

In the rear-view mirror, I saw Ralph look out of the window. Suddenly he started arching his back as if he was trying to get out of the car seat.

'Whoop!' he shouted. 'Whoop! Whoop!'

Before I could say anything, he raised his hands and threw the two toy cars at me. They bounced off the dashboard and landed in the footwell of the front passenger seat. It was sheer luck that they missed me and the windscreen. Thankfully I'd just turned the engine off otherwise I dread to think what could have happened.

I got out and went round and opened the car door.

'Ralph, we don't throw things, especially not in the car as it's very dangerous,' I told him firmly. 'If you throw the cars then it means you can't have them anymore.'

He stared at me but didn't say anything.

I lifted him out of the car and firmly grasped his hand as we walked towards the trolleys. Once I'd found one, I got Ralph to hold onto it as it would be tricky trying to do everything one-handed.

'Hold on tight, Ralph, please,' I told him.

I suspected I was on borrowed time so I had to do everything as quickly as I could. I went to the food section first and grabbed some sausages and a few basics like bread, milk and cereal.

'Good boy,' I told him, watching him like a hawk. 'Keep holding on nicely.'

So far, he'd been quiet and compliant.

'Let's go and get you a few clothes now,' I told him. 'You're doing really well.'

I quickly walked over to the boys' section and got some pants, socks and pyjamas in age six. As it was September, there weren't many shorts and T-shirts left so I knew I was going to have to sort through the sale rails to find anything in Ralph's size. I handed him one of the cars back to try and occupy him.

'Brumm brumm,' he muttered, running it up and down the side of the trolley.

'At last,' I sighed, finding a couple of T-shirts in his size at the back after a good rummage. 'Do you like them, Ralph?' I asked.

But when I turned back to the trolley, he wasn't there.

Panic surged through me. He'd been right next to me a few seconds ago but now there was no sign of him. I abandoned the trolley and went running up and down the aisles.

'Ralph!' I yelled frantically. 'Ralph, where are you?'

It was as if he'd vanished into thin air. My heart was racing and my chest felt so tight, I could barely breathe.

'Ralph, please answer me,' I shouted. 'If you're hiding, please come out.'

Where the heck was he?

I covered the whole clothing department but I couldn't see any sign of him. I ran over to a shop assistant.

'Have you seen a little boy?' I gasped. 'Brown hair, blue eyes, age six.'

I was giving her a description of the clothes that I'd put him in this morning so they could do an announcement over the Tannoy, when a woman walked past me.

'Absolutely disgusting,' she sighed. 'I blame the parents.'

I knew instinctively she was talking about Ralph.

I ran over to her.

'I've lost a little boy,' I panted. 'Have you seen him?'

'If you mean the child proudly peeing all over the floor in the toy aisle then yes,' she tutted.

I didn't let her finish before I ran off. I dashed through the store until I got to the toy section.

Please let it be him.

Sure enough, there was Ralph, shorts and pants around his ankles, doing a wee on the floor right in the middle of the toy aisle.

Thank goodness.

Other shoppers were tutting and shaking their heads and giving him a wide berth but I was just so relieved to see him. The first thing I did was pull up his shorts and pants.

I wasn't angry with him for weeing. It seemed to me that Ralph was normally used to weeing wherever he was, so I wasn't going to tell him off. However, I wanted to get through to him that he couldn't just run off.

'Ralph, we don't run off in the shop,' I told him firmly. 'You need to hold my hand or the trolley.'

'Cars,' he said, pointing to the shelves of toy cars. 'I like cars.'

'I know you do,' I replied. 'But you can't run off. That's not OK.'

Suddenly I was aware of the stares and the whispering around us and the large puddle of wee in the middle of the aisle. I knew we needed to get out of there as quickly as possible. Ignoring the dirty looks, I went to find the nearest shop assistant.

I found an older lady in the clothing section.

'I'm dreadfully sorry but we've had a bit of an accident in the toy aisle,' I told her.

'Oh, poor little lad,' she smiled sympathetically. 'Don't you worry, I'll get someone to sort it.'

I was so grateful for her kindness, I could have hugged her.

I'd grabbed enough clothes for now and I just wanted to get Ralph safely home. I walked him briskly to the checkout, holding his hand firmly onto the trolley. When we got there, I wedged him between the trolley and the till itself so he couldn't get out even if he wanted to.

'Is there somebody who could pack for me, please?' I asked the man on the till.

I wasn't prepared to take any chances or take my eyes off Ralph for a second and it was a relief when we got back to the car.

As soon as we got home, I knew one of the first things that we needed to master was the toilet. Ralph clearly knew what to do when someone took him to the toilet but he seemed to struggle to know when he needed to go to the toilet himself or to tell someone else, and just relieved himself wherever he was at the time. I knew that me and my house were not going to be able to cope with that.

Even with older children, the only way to teach this was to go right back to basics and use the timer like I did with toddlers. I'd set a timer on my phone or on a clock for every twenty minutes to remind me to take them to the toilet. Hopefully Ralph would start to recognise when he needed the loo and also learn that he always did it in the toilet.

As soon as we walked in the door, I set the timer. When it went off twenty minutes later, I marched him to the loo.

'Come on, Ralph, let's go for a wee.'

He did as I asked and when I saw him going to pull down his shorts, I half shut the door. I heard the tinkling in the toilet and then he came to the door.

'Did you flush it?' I asked him.

He looked at me blankly so I went in to show him.

'Remember what I showed you this morning?' I told him. 'You push down on this and it washes the wee away.'

Ralph looked terrified and as I pressed the flush, he edged back towards the door.

'Good job, Maggie!' I clapped. 'Now it's Ralph's turn.'

He shook his head.

'Come and have a go,' I told him.

I went over and led him towards the toilet. As I put his hand on the flush, I could feel that he was shaking.

'See,' I smiled. 'You've made the toilet nice and clean. Well done. Do you want to press it again and have a play with it?'

He shook his head.

I could see that he was still hesitant. I didn't know what it was that scared him about the flush but I knew I needed to get him used to it. Afterwards, I helped him to wash his hands. Then I reset the timer for it all to happen again in another twenty minutes.

Eventually I would learn how often he needed to go to the toilet so I could eventually ditch the timer and remind him. In the meantime, I also watched him like a hawk for any signs that he was about to pull down his shorts and pants. When I eventually found out more about his school, I'd talk to his teachers about it too. I didn't know anything about his school at this point or whether he was even in mainstream education.

Shelley arrived at my house just after lunch. She looked a lot less stressed and dishevelled than when I'd seen her the previous night.

'So how's it all going?' she asked me anxiously. 'How's Ralph getting on? Did he eventually settle down OK last night?'

'It's been quite a memorable time so far,' I told her.

I described how he had been tricky to get under control and how he'd lashed out at me with a dumper truck and it had left a mark. I talked about how he'd only had four hours' sleep and then he'd trashed both his own and Amena's bedrooms as well as running off in the supermarket.

'I'm so sorry to hear that,' she nodded. 'It's completely understandable perhaps when you think this is the third home he's been in in the past few days but it must have been very distressing for you.'

'It was,' I sighed. 'The hardest thing was seeing Amena so upset. She's such an easy-going, adaptable child and it was horrible that her things had been destroyed.'

Shelley suddenly looked panicked.

'Oh God, Maggie, you're not going to give notice on this placement, are you? I'd have no idea what to do next.'

'No, I'm not saying that,' I told her. 'I'm saying it has been exhausting and really hard work. I'm having to have a lot of physical contact with Ralph in terms of wrapping him in blankets and holding his hand whenever we're going anywhere to try to keep him safe.'

'Yes, I understand that,' she told me.

I also described how he'd weed and pooed everywhere.

'I suspect that's just what he's used to doing but I'm using the timer toilet training method and I'm hoping he'll quickly learn to go to the toilet.'

'Yes, that sounds sensible,' nodded Shelley.

'And then there's the whooping,' I added. 'He seems to do it when he's feeling anxious or out of control, which is understandably quite a lot at the moment.'

As I spoke, she made a note of what I was saying.

'It's been a bit of a shock but I could never give up on a child so soon,' I told her. 'He's already been passed from pillar to post – I wouldn't want to put him through any more upheaval.'

I still hardly knew anything about him and I was intrigued to know why he was behaving the way he was.

'So what can you tell me about Ralph and why he's come into care?' I asked.

Shelley described how three days ago, Ralph had been at school when he'd hit a teacher.

'He only started at the school four months ago when they moved to the area,' said Shelley. 'Apparently he's been a real handful. His teacher said he's very quiet and withdrawn but then has these huge outbursts when he destroys things and lashes out at other children.'

'What about Mum or Dad?' I asked.

Shelley explained that the school thought there was a stepdad around although they'd never seen him. They'd seen Mum a few times at the beginning but they hadn't managed to get hold of her.

'They've been calling her about Ralph's behaviour but she never answers and she hasn't got back to them. When he hit the teacher the other day, it was the final straw and they were thinking about excluding him or talking to Mum about specialist provision but again no one could get hold of her.'

'How on earth has he been getting to and from school then if Mum's not been around?' I asked.

'A neighbour of theirs at the block of flats where Ralph lives has been doing the pick-ups and drop-offs for the past few weeks,' Shelley explained. 'It transpires that Ralph had just sort of turned up at her door one morning in school uniform. The flats are a two-minute walk from the school so he'd tagged along with her and her kids and it carried on from there.

'School had checked with Mum and she'd signed a form that the neighbour brought in to say it was OK. Ralph's teacher had a word with the neighbour the other day at drop-off and it was only then that she admitted that she hadn't been able to get hold of Mum either. The flat was empty and Mum wasn't picking up her phone, so the neighbour had had Ralph for the past couple of nights.'

'But she hadn't said anything to anyone?' I asked, surprised.

'It's one of those communities where Social Services and social workers are seen as the enemy,' sighed Shelley. 'Bex, the neighbour, has been involved with Social Services herself in the past and, as she said to me, you don't grass people up to the Social. I think she just assumed that Mum would eventually turn up.'

As soon as Ralph's teacher had talked to Bex and found out what had happened, they'd immediately called in Social Services.

'The neighbour's got four children of her own so she couldn't have him long term and with no other family around and no contact made with Mum or Dad, he was taken into care.'

Ralph had initially come into the care system under what was known as an Emergency Protection Order or an EPO. It was issued by the courts for children who they felt were in immediate danger or, in Ralph's case, had been abandoned by their parent or caregiver.

'What happened with the other foster carers?' I asked.

Shelley shrugged.

She explained that at the first carer's house, Ralph had lashed out at another foster child.

'I think the second one had a very similar experience to you – wee and poo everywhere, very destructive behaviour – and they quickly decided that Ralph was going to be too much of a challenge for them and he needed to be moved on,' she nodded.

'Has he asked about his mum or dad or when he's going to go home?' asked Shelley.

'Not a thing,' I sighed. 'So what happens now?'

'All we can do is keep trying to get in touch with Mum,' shrugged Shelley 'I've left messages on her phone, put a note through the door of the flat, sent a letter. I've also asked Bex, the neighbour, to keep an eye out for her. We're also going through the benefits office to see if we can trace her that way and we've logged it with the police in case there are concerns about her safety.'

All I could think was no wonder this poor boy was in a state of complete confusion and fear. No matter what his home life had been like, to suddenly find everything that he knew had disappeared overnight and to have been abandoned not only by his parents but by two different carers must have been terrifying for him.

SIX

The Sanctuary of School

Before Shelley left, there was more we needed to discuss.

'What about school?' I asked. 'I know Ralph's had so much upheaval over the past few days but I think it would be good for him to have a little bit of normality.'

But I didn't even know if his school would be willing to have him back as before his parents had gone AWOL, they'd been talking about excluding him.

'I've spoken to Miss Loughran, the headteacher, and, given the circumstances, she's happy for Ralph to come back in,' Shelley told me. 'I think it would be really useful for you and I to have a chat to Ralph's class teacher both to fill her in on what's happening and to talk about how we're going to deal with his behaviour going forward.'

'That sounds like a good idea,' I added. 'I'd like to get more of a picture about how he is at school.'

As it was a Friday, we agreed that Ralph would start back at school the following Monday and we would go in that morning and chat to his teacher too.

*

Thankfully, despite that first horrendous night, Ralph slept OK the following evening. However, I noticed he had a habit of waking up early and repeatedly opening and closing his bedroom door.

So when I heard the same thudding sound on Saturday morning, I got out of bed and walked down the landing. I found Ralph standing at his bedroom door, open and closing it. I was unsure about how long he had actually been there for.

'Door open,' he told me.

'Yes,' I smiled. 'I always leave your door open a little bit so you can see the landing light or go to the toilet. If you're awake, flower, you know you can call me or come and get me – you don't have to wait.'

I didn't want to encourage him to go on a rampage like he had the day before but equally I didn't want him to think that he had to stay in his room.

After I'd reminded him to go to the toilet, we went downstairs for breakfast. I got the boxes of cereal out so Ralph could choose which one he wanted, along with some bowls and spoons.

Shortly afterwards, Amena wandered down in her pyjamas. Unlike most teenagers, she wasn't one for sleeping in.

'Fancy a bit of breakfast, flower?' I asked and she nodded.

I couldn't help but notice that Amena chose to sit at the opposite end of the table, as far away from Ralph as possible.

Ralph tucked into his bowl of Cheerios with great gusto. He was a messy eater and what I liked to call a 'wriggle bottom'. He was half on the chair, half off it, and never sat still but he always managed to get that spoon into his mouth. I didn't pull him up on it as I assumed that eating at the table and having regular mealtimes was probably a new thing and something he was still getting used to. The fact he was at the table and staying there was a win in my book at this early stage.

I was just putting some bread in the toaster when, out of the corner of my eye, I saw Ralph suddenly raise his hand and sweep his bowl and spoon off the table. Amena's mouth gaped open in shock as it smashed on the floor and milk splashed everywhere. Then he did the same to the open box of cereal so there were Cheerios all over the floor too.

'All gone,' he said matter-of-factly.

'You might have finished, Ralph, but we don't throw things on the floor,' I told him firmly.

Amena looked horrified.

'I'm going to my room,' she huffed, getting up and leaving the table.

I didn't make a big deal of it. I was confused about why he'd done it – I didn't feel as if he'd done it out of anger or frustration. But from then on, I decided that I would only give Ralph plastic plates and bowls to eat off in the future.

'Come on, let's get the dustpan and brush and clean it up,' I told him.

I handed it to him and he held the dustpan while I swept the Cheerios up.

'Open the bin for me please,' I said and he did as I'd asked, then I mopped up the milk with a cloth.

'Remember, we don't throw things,' I reiterated. 'We can't use that bowl now because it's all gone.'

'All gone,' he nodded.

Amena spent the rest of the morning in her bedroom. She was a typical teenager in that she liked hanging out in her room but at the weekend she'd normally come and watch TV with me or we'd be in the kitchen together chatting or doing some baking. But since Ralph had arrived, I'd noticed that she was deliberately keeping out of the way and I'd seen the way she'd reacted to him this morning.

While Ralph was playing with his beloved cars, I went up to her room to talk to her.

'I haven't seen much of you today,' I told her, sitting down on the end of her bed. 'Are you OK? It feels like you're trying to avoid Ralph.'

'I'm not being mean, Maggie, but I don't want to be near him,' she shrugged. 'He's dirty and he acts weird and he does horrible things.'

I completely understood where she was coming from. The dynamics of our whole house had changed with Ralph's arrival.

'I know it's hard,' I told her. 'And I know it was really horrible for you when he went into your room and destroyed your things, but we've got to remember that he's probably come from a home that is very different to this one and he's just adjusting and learning a whole new set of rules.'

'But why does he do such nasty things?' she asked.

'I don't think he's being deliberately nasty,' I explained. 'I don't fully know yet why he behaves like this, but we've all got to be patient while we get used to each other.'

'But I don't want to get used to him if he's gonna do this stuff,' she replied.

'I'm sure things will get better as Ralph settles in,' I added.

It was always hard, especially as a single carer, when a new child arrived – there was always a period of adjustment. Ralph was taking up all of my attention although I tried to make sure Amena had some time with me after he'd gone to bed. I hoped that, in time, she would come round to him as he settled in.

That afternoon, I'd invited my friend Vicky round. Like me, she'd been a foster carer for over twenty years although we worked for different agencies. She'd been fostering a group of three brothers – six-year-old Grant, John, ten, and Robert, thirteen. Their biological parents were both alcoholics and they'd witnessed domestic violence at home. Vicky had had to deal with some really challenging behaviour, especially from the older two boys, and it had been a struggle as she was a single carer like me. However, they'd started to calm down and Vicky had become really attached to them. She was even about to apply for a Special Guardianship Order, which meant there would be no more Social Services involvement and she would have parental responsibility for them all until they were eighteen. But then, just over seven months ago, Robert had made a serious allegation against Vicky. He'd told a teacher that she'd lost her temper a couple of times and slapped him. Vicky was adamant that it had never happened. The boys had been immediately removed from her care and had gone to live with another carer and Vicky hadn't seen them since.

It was the most horrific thing to go through and it had been horrendous to see my friend so broken. The police had said there were no criminal charges for her to answer to, which had been a huge relief, but Social Services were still carrying out their investigations. It was taking so long and the effect on Vicky's life had been catastrophic. Until the results of the investigation were known, Vicky wasn't allowed to foster any other children so she'd lost all of her income overnight. As a single woman with a mortgage to pay, she had been terrified. Through a loan from a family member and working in a shop, she was just about getting by but it had been a devastating time for her.

I knew Vicky and the kind of person and carer she was, and I was convinced the allegation was something she would never ever do. It had been so hard to see her go through losing the boys and her livelihood and there was always the awareness that this could happen to any of us. The allegations also meant that I couldn't leave any of my children in Vicky's care although she could still come round and see us. I made sure we still met up regularly and I'd told her about Ralph.

When she arrived, he was playing with the cars.

'That's not what I was expecting,' she commented in a quiet voice. 'He seems very chilled.'

'The cars are the one thing that really calm him but I still have to watch him like a hawk,' I told her. 'Things can suddenly flip and then he's running around destroying things or pooing on the floor.'

'How is the toilet training going?' she asked.

'We're slowly cracking it,' I replied. 'He knows exactly what to do when someone takes him to the toilet, which I'm guessing perhaps has been taught to him at school. But, left to his own devices, he just goes wherever he wants to. He's not keen on the flush either.'

Vicky seemed to have a natural affinity with most children and before long she was lying down on the kitchen floor playing cars with Ralph.

While he lined them up, she made revving noises and drove some cars around the road mat that I'd dug out of the loft.

'Ooh, I like this sports car,' she said, picking up a white Ferrari.

'No!' shouted Ralph sternly, snatching it off her. 'My car!'

He raised his hand and slammed the car down on Vicky's arm.

'Are you OK?' I asked her.

'I'm fine,' she said. 'Honestly.'

I went over to Ralph and took the cars off him.

'Ralph, we don't hit people,' I told him. 'And if you do, you won't be allowed to play with the cars anymore.'

'No!' he said.

He kicked the line of cars that he'd made, sending them scattering everywhere, then tipped up the plastic box and the rest of them fell out all over the floor. Then he ran through the open patio doors and out into the garden.

'I see what you mean about things changing quickly,' said Vicky.

We watched him through the patio doors, running round in circles and whooping.

'I don't think his behaviour is just a reaction to his home life and being taken into care,' I told Vicky. 'I definitely think he needs to be assessed for additional needs.'

There was the whooping and the meltdowns as well as the fact he wasn't as verbal as he should be at the age of six.

'Why does he run like that?' wondered Vicky.

'Run like what?' I asked.

'He sort of runs in a lopsided way with his leg turned in,' she replied.

I suppose up to that point, I'd never really watched Ralph run, except the night he'd arrived and he'd had his pants and trousers around his ankles, which was bound to make him move differently.

'I've not noticed it before, to be honest, but there are a lot of things about Ralph that I want to get checked out. I'm going to talk to his school and the GP about a possible autism assessment – I'll ask them to check his leg then.'

'It's probably nothing,' nodded Vicky.

On Sunday, I tried to keep things as quiet as possible ahead of Ralph's first day back at school. I talked to him about school and found out that his teacher was called Mrs White. He obviously liked the routine of it because he'd managed to get himself ready every day when he was going to school with Bex the neighbour.

Shelley had visited again and managed to get a school uniform for Ralph, which he recognised straight away.

'School!' he said, when he saw me hanging it up in his wardrobe.

She had picked up a school book bag for him too and he was clearly delighted with it. He looked at it in amazement and kept touching it.

'Do you like your school bag?' I asked him.

He nodded.

'School bag,' he repeated. 'I like my school bag.'

'That's good,' I smiled. 'You can take it to school tomorrow and show Mrs White. She's looking forward to seeing you.'

I was worried that on Monday morning, when it actually came to taking him to school, he was going to have a massive meltdown so I set my alarm for half an hour earlier than I usually did to give us more time. By 6 a.m. I heard the telltale thud of Ralph opening and closing his bedroom door.

When I went to see him, he was standing at the door.

'Put it on,' he said, pointing to his uniform.

'You want to get dressed now?' I asked him and he nodded eagerly.

Getting Ralph dressed was always a battle but this was the first time he was letting me put clothes on him and he was even putting them on himself. It was obvious he knew what he was doing and it was familiar to him.

Still quiet and calm, Ralph had breakfast and went willingly in the car. Even though the morning had gone like a dream, I didn't want to take any chances and I held his hand tightly as we walked across the playground to his classroom.

Mrs White was there to meet us. She was a dark-haired woman in her thirties who was heavily pregnant.

'Hi, Ralph,' she smiled. 'It's good to see you back.'

He didn't say anything but he walked calmly into the classroom.

'I'll just get the class settled and then the TA can take over. I'll come and meet you and the social worker in reception,' she told me.

I walked to the reception desk to sign myself in. Shelley was already waiting.

'How was Ralph this morning?' she asked warily. 'I hope it wasn't too much of a nightmare.'

'Amazingly, he was quiet and calm and did everything that I asked.'

'He sounds like a different child,' nodded Shelley.

'I think he was pleased about coming to school,' I said.

Mrs White came out to meet us a few minutes later and we went into a little office. She eased herself down onto the chair.

'Congratulations,' I smiled. 'When's your baby due?'

'I've still got three months left but I suddenly feel massive,' she sighed.

A receptionist brought us all in a cup of tea.

'So what can you tell us about Ralph?' asked Shelley.

'How can I put this?' she told us. 'He's only been at the school for a matter of months but, to be honest, he's been a challenge.'

'There have been issues from the beginning,' she continued. 'He would regularly go to the toilet in the classroom or in the playground so we have had to teach him how to use the loo. He's fine if someone takes him but he still often relieves himself wherever he is.

'Unfortunately, myself and the TA just don't have the time to be taking him to the toilet every fifteen minutes.'

'That's something I've been working with him on over the past few days so hopefully things will start to improve,' I told her.

We also talked about Ralph's behaviour.

'He can be very quiet and withdrawn but then he also has these massive meltdowns,' Mrs White added. 'And over the past few months, they have been getting progressively worse. There have been a couple of instances recently where I've had to leave the classroom with the other pupils as he's been pushing tables over, emptying out all the cupboards and literally trashing the place so I haven't felt it's been safe for us to be around him.'

I nodded.

'And you haven't had any success in contacting his parents?' Shelley asked as she made notes.

'No,' shrugged Mrs White. 'I used to see Mum in the playground a while ago but she'd be there one minute, gone the next and I never managed to grab her. I've left voicemails, emails, posted letters, given Ralph letters to take home – but I've heard nothing.'

She described the incident the previous week when Ralph had lashed out in the playground and hit a supervisor.

'I spoke to the headteacher and I knew we'd reached a point where we really needed to speak to Mum about possibly excluding Ralph for a couple of days and whether alternative provision might be a better option for him.'

'Did you ever think about contacting Social Services about him?' asked Shelley.

'Our school is in a deprived area,' Mrs White told us. 'We have lots of kids who come to school in tatty, dirty uniforms who are hungry and never have breakfast.

'In the time I've known him, Ralph has always been here on time every day and in his uniform, even though it was grubby and smelly. He wasn't especially underweight so I believed he was being fed at home and he had free school meals when he was here.'

She described how last week things had taken a turn for the worse.

'We're used to parents not turning up for parents' evenings or replying to school trip letters or phone calls, but we had reached crunch point in terms of Ralph's behaviour where we needed to do something and we'd drawn a blank in contacting Mum.'

'When's the last time you saw her?' asked Shelley.

'It's probably quite a few weeks since she's picked him up,' replied Mrs White. 'You don't tend to notice on a morning as the children line up in the playground and the parents often drop them off and leave straight away if they're heading to work.

'But it's been predominantly Kirby's mum who's been there at pick-up. I just assumed Mum had a new job or something. It was only when I spoke to Kirby's mum last week about urgently needing to speak to Ralph's mum that she admitted that Ralph's mum had been AWOL for a couple of days. Obviously when I found that out, I went straight to the head and we called in Social Services straight away.'

Shelley nodded.

'I know he's only been with me a few days but he strikes me as a child who could have some sort of additional needs,' I told her. 'Has he been assessed for anything?'

'I completely agree,' replied Mrs White. 'That's another thing we wanted to discuss with Mum but we need her permission to take it any further.'

'I was going to talk to the GP about it too,' I nodded.

'We can definitely give permission for that,' added Shelley.

'Let's keep in contact about Ralph's behaviour then, Maggie,' said Mrs White.

'Absolutely,' I nodded. 'If there are any huge meltdowns at school then please ring me and let me know. And we can have a quick catch-up at pick-up each day.'

Shelley confirmed that I would be the only one picking

Ralph up from school and that I could sign for any school permissions.

'Have you managed to get hold of Ralph's parents yet?' Mrs White asked.

'Not as yet,' replied Shelley. 'But we're working with the police to try and trace them.'

'Fingers crossed,' she said.

As we came out of school, Shelley and I chatted as we walked to our cars.

'As it's been nearly a week now without any contact from Mum or the stepdad and they're not replying to messages or letters, the police have said they're going to force entry to the flat,' she told me. 'I think they just want to double-check that there are no suspicious circumstances or that they haven't come to any harm.'

'Gosh, I really hope not,' I shuddered.

'They've said I can go with them, just in case Mum is there and just not answering the door – I'm going to head over there now.'

'Let me know how it goes,' I said to her.

With both Ralph and Amena at school, I headed home to catch up on some cleaning and paperwork. It was just after lunch when I heard a knock at the door.

I was surprised to see Shelley standing there.

'I'm sorry to call without letting you know,' she told me.

'Don't be silly,' I replied. 'Come in. Did you go to the flat with the police?'

She nodded her head and I could see that she looked visibly upset.

I led her through to the kitchen and made her a cup of tea.

'What happened?' I asked. 'Was it that bad?'

She nodded again.

'I've been doing this job for over fifteen years and it never ceases to amaze me how some people live,' she sighed, taking a big swig of tea. 'It's just so upsetting, Maggie. You wouldn't keep an animal in those conditions, never mind a child.'

As Shelley described what they had found, all I could think about was little Ralph. My heart broke for him and for how he had been forced to live.

'It was so cluttered,' she sighed. 'You could barely get in the front door for the mess and the rubbish.'

She described how there had been drug paraphernalia everywhere, overflowing ashtrays, empty bottles of alcohol and mountains of rubbish.

'You couldn't see the work surfaces in the kitchen or the sink as there was so much stuff. Takeaway containers that were obviously weeks old with maggots in them, crisp packets, Pot Noodles, biscuits, empty cans of beans all just discarded on the floor.

'The whole place stank and was filthy,' she sighed. 'There were flies and poo and wee everywhere. They've been living in utter squalor.'

'Did Ralph have a bedroom?' I asked.

'He had a bed but it was a tiny toddler-sized one. There were no sheets on it, just an old blanket and the whole thing was soiled and covered in excrement. It was even up the walls in his room, Maggie.'

She described how there had been rubbish and empty food wrappers all over his floor.

'It's as if he ate something and just threw the packaging or wrapper down, and the carpet was disgusting and smelt of wee. There was no light in his room, not even a light bulb in the empty fitting, and no curtains.

'But that wasn't all. There was a big padlock on the outside of his bedroom door,' she sighed. 'He's clearly been locked in there for long periods of time.

'There were scratch marks and little holes all up the inside of the door,' continued Shelley. 'The poor little lad had been trying to claw his way out.'

'Perhaps that explains where the poo smearing could have come from,' I shrugged.

I'd known children who had done it in the past and it was often something they did out of devastating boredom when they had no interaction with anyone for hours on end and no toys to play with.

It also suddenly made sense as to why Ralph was always opening and closing his bedroom door at my house. He was probably checking to see if he was locked in.

Sadly it was something that I had experienced before. I'd fostered a baby once whose parents had put a large piece of wood over the top of his cot so he couldn't climb out.

'So there was no sign of the parents?' I asked.

'None at all,' said Shelley. 'But no sign that they had come to any harm. To be honest, Maggie, I wasn't in there for long. The smell was so bad and I'd seen enough.'

It was heartbreaking to hear but it explained a lot. Suddenly Ralph had gone from a home where there were no rules, except for the chance he could be locked in a room when his caregivers had had enough of him, to a home where he was subject to boundaries and expectations. He'd been transported to a whole different world and that's a huge adjustment for any child, let alone suddenly not seeing your parents and not being able to say goodbye. It was no wonder he had these moments of meltdowns and anxiety.

It's always terribly sad when you hear that a child has had to live like that but I had to focus on my mantra. I always told myself that I couldn't change the past for children like Ralph, I could only help them move forward. I had to focus on what was to happen next for Ralph and try to make his life as stable and comfortable as possible until we worked out what we could do for him.

SEVEN

Playground Showdown

A whole week had now passed with Ralph at my house. School was definitely helping to give him some sense of normality and routine.

There were still meltdowns and challenging behaviour but they were slightly less frequent, partly, I think, because Ralph seemed very tired when he got home.

Every afternoon at pick-up, I'd have a chat with Mrs White and she would fill me in on the day and how Ralph had been. I could see how relieved she was to have some input and someone to share it all with at last.

One afternoon I was there as usual to collect Ralph. I made my way across the crowded playground to his classroom while parents and children milled around and chatted in the sun. I liked to time it so I got there towards the end of pick-up, so it was easier for Mrs White to talk to me as most of the other pupils had already been collected or gone to after-school club. I could see Ralph through the window waiting inside the classroom.

'Hi, Ralph,' I waved as I hovered outside the door.

He gave me a shy smile as he came running out.

'Maggie, I'm pleased to say that Ralph's had a really good day today,' Mrs White smiled. 'Haven't you, Ralph?'

'Oh, that's great,' I grinned. 'Well done, flower.'

But before I had a chance to ask why, I suddenly heard a commotion in the playground behind me. Someone was shouting.

'Oi!' a woman's voice yelled. 'What are you doing with my f***ing kid? Get your hands off him.'

It was only when I heard what she said next that my heart sank.

'Ralph, it's Mum. Get here now!'

I spun around. The crowd of parents and pupils parted as a couple marched across the playground straight towards us. The only word I could use to describe the woman was ravaged. She was probably in her early thirties but her face was hollow and grey and covered in spots and scabs. Her hair was thin and greasy and her skeletal body was swamped by a filthy T-shirt and holey leggings. The man with her was equally as thin and pale. He was wearing a dirty hoodie and a baseball cap that failed to disguise a black eye and a weeping cut on his face. They both looked like they hadn't slept or washed in days.

Ralph's mum and stepdad.

I glanced at Ralph who was frozen to the spot by my side and I put my arm on his shoulder to reassure him.

'It's OK,' I said gently. 'Don't worry. I'll sort this out.'

He looked up at me and then suddenly he ran. At first I thought he was going to his mum but he started running around in circles at the side of the playground.

'Whoop! Whoop!' he yelled, with his fingers in his ears. 'Whoop! Whoop!'

'F***ing weirdo,' sighed his stepdad. 'Ralph, come 'ere now. You're coming with me and your mum.'

'Whoop!' yelled Ralph.

I turned to Mrs White, who looked completely panicked and unsure of what to do. I knew I had to act fast to get Ralph out of the way and diffuse the situation as quickly as possible.

'Please could you take Ralph back into the classroom for me and ask the head if she could come out here ASAP?' I asked her.

'Er, yes, yes, of course,' she muttered.

I ran over to Ralph, put my arm around him and, firmly but gently, steered him over to Mrs White.

'You go with Mrs White while I have a chat to your parents,' I told him. 'Good boy.'

She just managed to scoop him out of the way and into the nearest classroom before his mum got to us.

'I said, what the f*** do you think you're doing?' she yelled in my face, spraying me with spit and a blast of rancid breath. 'He's my kid and he does what I say.'

Her eyes were glassy and bloodshot. Her teeth were brown and I could see she was missing a couple at the front.

'Renae, my name's Maggie,' I explained.

I didn't even have a chance to finish.

'I don't care what your f***ing name is!' she yelled. 'You're a f***ing child snatcher!'

I could feel myself shaking but I had to stay calm. I also knew I couldn't go into any details about Ralph's case in such a public situation in front of other parents and pupils.

'I'm just a foster carer,' I told her in a low voice. 'I was asked by Social Services to look after Ralph. You need to get in touch with his social worker Shelley and she will be able to explain the situation to you and tell you what's happening. If you give me two minutes then I can get you her number.'

My hands were trembling as I rummaged through my bag looking for a pen and paper.

'Forget it!' Renae spat. 'I ain't talking to anyone from the Social. He's my kid, he's coming with me.'

Ralph's stepdad, Dean, was standing there too. His nose was running and he kept wiping it on the sleeve of his hoodie. I could see his pupils were dilated.

'Bring the kid out now,' he threatened. 'Or do I have to go and get him myself?'

Renae had clearly decided that she wanted to make as big a scene as possible.

'Somebody help me!' she shouted at the top of her lungs. 'This b**** is trying to steal my kid!'

Dean started laughing.

Thankfully, just at that moment, back-up arrived. The head-teacher came dashing out. I'd never met her before.

'I'm Miss Loughran, the headteacher here,' she explained to the couple. 'We are acting under instruction from Social Services. Ralph is currently only permitted to be picked up by Ms Hartley, so I'm afraid he won't be going with you. If you want to come inside into my office then I'm happy to get Ralph's social worker on the phone and she can clarify that for you.'

I was so relieved that she was clearly trying to diffuse the situation and get Renae and Dean out of the playground and into somewhere more private.

'I told you, we ain't talking to anyone from the Social,' sighed Renae. 'He's my kid and he's coming with us. Dean, go and get him.'

Miss Loughran was small in stature but she was a formidable force.

'The way I see it, you've got two choices,' she told them firmly. 'You can either come into my office and we can have a sensible discussion about this or you can leave the premises.'

'She ain't leaving here without her kid,' said Dean.

'Yeah, he ain't going with this stupid b****,' sneered Renae, gesturing at me.

'Well, then, I'm afraid I have no other option than to call the police and they will help you to leave the premises,' said Miss Loughran calmly. 'I can't let Ralph go with you.'

At the mention of 'police', Renae shot Dean a concerned look.

'I ain't talking to no pigs,' he told her. 'Come on, let's go.'

Renae looked at me.

'You haven't seen the last of me,' she sneered. 'I'll be back and next time I'm gonna be taking my boy with me.'

Dean gave us a menacing look and then spat on the floor next to Miss Loughran's feet before he and Renae marched off across the playground.

I held my breath until they'd walked out of the front gates and disappeared off down the street.

'Well, that was unpleasant,' sighed Miss Loughran. 'I'm so sorry you had to go through that. I was on the phone and had no idea what was going on until Mrs White came running into my office. Are you OK?'

'I think so,' I muttered.

'Let's go and check on Ralph and then I think we could both do with a strong cup of tea.'

'Thank you,' I said gratefully.

I was still feeling very shaky as we walked over to the classroom. But I knew I had to put my feelings to one side as my priority was making sure that Ralph was OK. I didn't know how he would be feeling after seeing his parents.

We went into the classroom where Mrs White had taken him. There were books and toys all over the floor and it was clear that Ralph had been on one of his rampages.

'I couldn't stop him,' she sighed. 'I tried but he was kicking and lashing out.'

'Poor lad,' I nodded. 'It's understandable.'

I knew this was probably his way of expressing some of the stress and panic that he'd felt at seeing his parents storming into the playground like that.

I went over to him and put my hand on his.

'Ralph, it's OK,' I told him. 'Your mum has gone now. Come and sit down and I'm sure Mrs White will get you a drink.'

'Drink?' he said.

'Yes, Ralph, I can get you a beaker of milk,' she nodded.

I held his hand and led him over to a chair. He seemed a lot calmer now and he sat down and had a drink.

'Miss Loughran's gone to make me a cup of tea but when she gets back, I think you and I need to do some tidying up in here,' I told him, looking round the classroom that he'd just trashed.

'No!' he said, shaking his head and throwing the empty plastic beaker onto the floor.

I ignored him and started putting things back into boxes. At first he just watched and then eventually he came over and started putting some LEGO into a plastic box.

'Good boy,' I told him. 'You're doing a great job.'

We tidied away side by side.

As I was putting some dolls into a box, Ralph turned to me.

'Mum gone?' he asked.

He had such a forlorn, confused look on his face and my heart broke for him.

'Yes,' I nodded. 'Your mum's gone.'

'Mum come back?' he asked me.

'Not today,' I replied. 'You're going to sleep at Maggie's house until Shelley works out what's happening.'

'Sleep at Maggie's house?' he repeated and I nodded.

By the time we'd tidied up, it was 4.15 p.m.

'We'd best be getting home,' I said.

'Just to be on the safe side, do you want me to walk you out to your car just to make sure they're not still hanging around outside?' Miss Loughran suggested.

'Yes, that would be great,' I said.

Even though there were three of us, I still felt really anxious as we walked out of the school entrance. I could see Ralph looking around nervously too.

'I think it would be a good idea in future if you came to pick up Ralph ten or fifteen minutes before the bell goes,' Miss Loughran suggested. 'Just in case they turn up again.'

'That makes sense,' I nodded.

I really didn't want the same thing happening again.

'As soon as I get home, I'll phone Ralph's social worker and let her know what's happened,' I told her.

'OK,' she nodded.

Ralph was very quiet on the journey home and he looked exhausted. I spent the whole time looking anxiously in my mirrors, checking there was no one following us. And when we got home, I scanned the street to make sure there was no one lurking around. These kinds of incidents left me constantly looking over my shoulder.

When we walked into the kitchen, Amena was there eating some toast.

'You're back late,' she said.

'Oh, the traffic was terrible,' I smiled, putting down my keys.

I got Ralph settled with the cars as I knew they were his happy place and he was always calm when he played with them.

I went upstairs and called Shelley straight away.

'We had a bit of an issue at school pick-up today,' I told her.

I explained what had happened.

'Oh, Maggie, I'm so sorry about that,' Shelley told me. 'That must have been horrible for you.'

'These things happen,' I replied. 'But it was really intimidating and I was worried about poor Ralph.'

It was always a really uncomfortable feeling when a birth parent publicly accused you of all sorts as it was impossible to defend yourself without breaching confidentiality. Also, I didn't want to open up a dialogue with Renae. It wasn't the right place or time.

'How's Ralph?' she asked.

'He seems very anxious and confused,' I told her. 'I've tried to explain it to him but I don't know how much he understands.'

I also asked what would happen with Renae and Dean now.

'I tried to give Renae your phone number but she wasn't having any of it,' I added.

'Well, now I know that they're around again, I'm going to call at the flat and see if I can catch them,' Shelley told me. 'In fact, as soon as I put the phone down, I'm going to go there.'

'Will they be arrested?' I asked.

'I'm not sure,' replied Shelley. 'We're in touch with the police and updating them – it's up to them to decide if they're going to face any criminal charges.'

Technically they had abandoned Ralph without making an arrangement for him, but because Bex had stepped in to look after him, he hadn't actually been left on his own. If she hadn't found out they had gone, things could have been very different. Given the state of the flat and how Ralph had been living, there would also be a question about whether they would be charged with child neglect.

That evening, Ralph was very quiet and clingy. Wherever I went, he followed me. I went into the living room to get a mug Amena had left in there and I turned round to find Ralph behind me, clutching a car in each hand.

'You're like my little shadow tonight,' I told him.

Shelley called me just as I was making tuna pasta for tea.

'How did it go at the flat?' I asked.

'No one answered the door unfortunately,' she replied. 'I don't know if there was anyone there and they just didn't answer or whether they genuinely weren't around. I hung around for a while but I didn't hear or see anything so I put another letter through the door stating that Ralph is now in the care of the local authority and that they need to contact me for more information and to arrange to see him. The letter also makes it clear that if they return to school at any point to pick up Ralph then the police will be called.'

I just hoped that it was enough to stop them turning up at school because I knew both Ralph and I couldn't face going through that again.

EIGHT

Aftershock

Looking at Ralph lying in bed that night, my heart went out to him.

I still felt shaken up by what had happened in the school playground, so I couldn't even imagine how he must be feeling and what must be going through that little mind of his.

As I was tucking him in, he turned to me.

'Sleep at Maggie's house,' he said in a quiet voice.

'Yes,' I nodded. 'You're going to sleep at Maggie's.'

I reached my hand out to gently stroke his hair but he ducked out of the way. I'd noticed he wasn't a particularly affectionate child and didn't like being touched, and I wasn't going to push that. All I could do was keep reassuring him and hope that he understood that he was safe.

As I walked downstairs, I felt an overwhelming sense of sadness for this little boy and what he'd been through. Sadly he didn't have the words to explain it all to us yet, even if he wanted to.

Amena was sat in the living room watching TV.

'I'll come and sit with you in a minute, lovey,' I told her wearily. 'I've just got to send some emails.'

'That's OK,' she said. 'My mum's going to call me now.'

While Amena chatted to her mum, I wrote up everything that had happened at school in my recordings and sent a copy to Becky, my supervising social worker.

Ten minutes after I pressed 'send', she called me.

'I wouldn't usually ring this late but I've just read your message,' she told me. 'I'm so sorry about what happened today at school – it must have been really scary. Are you all right? It's really uncomfortable when those sort of confrontations with parents happen.'

'It was horrible,' I said. 'They were really kicking off and I was worried that it was going to turn really nasty and we'd have to call the police. Plus I was aware that Ralph was there and witnessing it all, although we managed to get him into a classroom pretty quickly.'

I knew I could offload to Becky and talk more honestly.

'Also, I just felt so embarrassed,' I said. 'I know that these things happen but it's mortifying when all of these other parents and kids are staring at you like you're some sort of kidnapper.'

'Are you worried about going to school tomorrow?' she asked.

We talked about what extra measures had been put in place to try to help us both feel more secure.

'I'm going to drop Ralph off ten minutes after the bell has gone and then pick him up ten minutes early,' I told her. 'Plus Shelley has sent another letter to Mum and Dad stating if they turn up at school again, the police will be called.'

'Hopefully that will do the trick,' said Becky, 'but if there are any more issues then let me know.'

Despite the new arrangements, I still felt anxious about doing the school run in the morning. When an incident like that happens with birth parents, it puts you on edge and I knew, at least for the next few days, I would be constantly looking over my shoulder.

I didn't sleep very well but thankfully for once Ralph did and it was 7.30 a.m. before I heard him at his bedroom door.

'Door open,' he told me as I went to see him.

'Yes, the door's always open at Maggie's house,' I reassured him.

When I walked in the room to open his blind, a pungent smell hit my nostrils. My heart sank when I saw a huge wet patch in the middle of the carpet.

'Ralph, have you done a wee on the floor?' I asked him. 'You know we do wees in the toilet.'

'Whoop! Whoop!' he shouted, running out of the door and down the landing.

I got an old towel from the bathroom and mopped up some of the wetness then I sprayed it with carpet cleaner. That would do for now; I'd tackle it properly while Ralph was at school.

Meanwhile, Ralph was still running up and down the landing.

'Ralph, come and get dressed for school,' I told him.

'No!' he said defiantly.

It's going to be one of those mornings, I thought to myself.

Since he'd gone back to school, he'd been really compliant when it came to getting ready in the morning. However, today was clearly going to be different, so I decided to change tactic.

'OK, let's go down for breakfast then,' I said cheerfully.

What followed could only be described as a battle of wills. Everything I asked him to do, Ralph pushed back.

He refused point-blank to sit at the table. I knew he was hungry and needed to eat something before school but sometimes you had to pick your battles, so I let him have his bowl of cereal sitting on the floor underneath the table.

When Amena came in and saw him, she rolled her eyes.

'I think it's going to be one of those days,' I told her quietly.

After he'd finished his breakfast, I was clearing everything away when I turned around to find Ralph pulling the heads off some pink roses that Louisa had bought me. She was thoughtful like that and often picked up a bunch of flowers for me when she did her supermarket shop.

'Ralph, please don't do that to my pretty flowers,' I told him. 'It will make me really sad.'

He looked me straight in the eye, picked up the vase and then threw it against the wall where it smashed to smithereens.

I was so shocked, I didn't know what to say.

Before I could stop him, Ralph picked up my favourite mug – a posh polka dot one that some adoptive parents had bought me years ago – and threw that too. Tea dripped down my kitchen walls.

I took a deep breath; it took all my inner strength to remain calm.

'We don't throw things,' I told him firmly. 'We're going upstairs to get dressed now.'

I knew the cars always calmed him so I grabbed a couple and then took his hand and led him upstairs. Ralph was having none of it. He tried to wriggle out of my grasp. Then he hung off my arm to the point that at one stage, I was almost dragging him down the landing.

'Ralph, please walk properly,' I told him. 'You're going to hurt yourself and me if you're not careful.'

Once we got to his bedroom, he started jumping on his bed then he leapt on top of the chest of drawers and the whooping started again.

All I could think was that this was his way of expressing his anxiety and stress about going to school after what had happened the previous day.

Eventually I managed to wrap him in a blanket and we sat on the bedroom floor.

'We need to get dressed for school now,' I told him.

'No!' he said. 'No! No! No!'

I handed him two cars – one for each hand. Normally he'd sit and study them but this time he hurled them across the room. Holding him between my legs, I tried to pull on what clothes I could. But Ralph wriggled and kicked and flexed his back and it was a huge struggle. I managed to get his pants and shorts on but he only had one sock on and his polo short was hanging around his neck when he broke free and ran off again.

OK, Ralph, have it your way, I thought.

If need be, I would take him to school like that and hopefully by the time we got there, he would have calmed down enough to allow me to help him get dressed properly. I did once look after a child who went to a special school and I'd had so much difficulty and stress getting them dressed one morning that I'd taken them in in their pyjamas. They'd soon got dressed when their teacher had asked them to!

I was absolutely exhausted and I hadn't even got Ralph in the car yet, but I was determined that he was going to go to school. I wanted to show him that, despite what had happened yesterday, school was a safe place. If I let him stay off, then the same behaviour would happen the following schoolday and it would just delay the inevitable.

Ralph refused to put his shoes on so I put them in the car and somehow I managed to get him into his car seat. At last, he sat there quietly.

Thank goodness, I thought to myself as I turned the key in the ignition and set off down the road.

As I looked in the rear-view mirror, I could see Ralph flexing in his seat and trying to fiddle with the buckle.

'Ralph, you need to sit still in the car,' I told him.

Suddenly I felt a sharp whack in my back that made me jump.

Whack.

And again.

I realised that Ralph was kicking my seat.

'You need to stop that please,' I told him.

I tried to distract him.

'What can you see out of the window?' I asked. 'Can you see any blue cars or what about a yellow one?'

'Whoop, whoop!' he yelled, kicking the back of my seat again.

I could feel my stress levels rising to new heights – I had to stay calm.

Suddenly there was an almighty bang and I could see that he was banging his fist against the car window which then, to my horror, was followed by his head.

'Ralph, you need to stop this now. If you carry on like this then I'm going to have to stop the car.'

But I didn't know if he could hear me above the loud whooping.

When I realised that he had somehow managed to undo the buckle in his seatbelt and was crouched down in the footwell, reaching up to pull my hair, it was the final straw.

I immediately pulled over.

'Ralph, I'm not driving this car until you get back in your car seat and let me strap you in,' I told him.

'No!' he shouted, banging the back of my seat with his fist.

We'd only got five minutes down the road. I sat in the front seat, utterly exhausted, and felt like bursting into tears.

I would have loved nothing more than to give up and take him home but I'd still have to get him in the car seat to do that, so I was still determined to get him to school.

I knew it was unsafe to carry on driving when he was behaving like this. The only way I could possibly start the car again was if I had someone to sit in the back with him.

I wracked my brains – I knew Vicky had an appointment with her solicitor that morning and my friend Carol had her own three foster kids to get ready for school. Then I remembered Louisa mentioning that she had a day off from her nannying job. I didn't want Edie to play any part in this but I also remembered that she'd started doing two mornings a week at nursery. I looked at the clock. It was after 9 a.m. and we were already late for school.

I gave her a call.

'Are you OK, Maggie?' she asked.

'Not really,' I said. 'I've got a bit of a situation and I wondered if you could help.'

I didn't go into details as Ralph could hear, but I think Louisa understood what I was implying.

'Of course, I can come and help,' she told me. 'I've just dropped Edie off at nursery so I was only going to go back and clean the flat.'

I told her where I'd pulled over.

'OK, I'm on my way,' she replied.

I was so grateful for the support network that I had around me, with Louisa and my friends. It was important as a foster carer to know you had trusted people whom you could turn to in a crisis.

While I waited for Louisa, I sat there in silence and didn't turn round or say anything to Ralph, who was still crouched in the footwell. I didn't want to give his behaviour any attention.

Ten minutes later, I was still feeling close to tears when I saw Louisa's car pull up behind mine in the quiet residential street.

'Thank you so much, lovey,' I said to her, my voice cracking.

'It's OK,' she said, giving me a hug. 'I'm happy to help.'

She took control of the situation and I was so grateful.

'Hello, Ralph,' she said, lifting him up from the footwell and back into his car seat. 'You can sit in the back with me and we'll get you to school. Your teacher must be wondering where you are.'

I don't know whether it was the fact that Louisa was someone new but Ralph let her strap him back in and I was finally able to start the car. She chatted to him all the way there and handed him a packet of raisins that she had in her handbag, which he ate.

Fifteen minutes later, I breathed a sigh of relief as we pulled up outside school.

'Do you want me to help you take him in?' asked Louisa.

'No, you stay here, flower, and I'll deal with this bit,' I told her.

Thankfully Ralph seemed to have calmed down a lot and I managed to coax him out of the car and through the school gates, although he kept looking anxiously around him. But as soon as we started walking across the empty playground, he broke free and started running around in circles and whooping.

Mrs White must have seen us through the window as she came out.

'Has it been a tricky morning?' she asked me.

'It's been a real struggle,' I nodded. 'I think his anxiety levels are high after what happened yesterday.'

'Don't worry, we can take it from here,' she told me kindly.

'Thank you,' I replied.

I said a quick goodbye to Ralph and then left.

As I walked back to the car, I felt completely broken. When I got back into the driver's seat, I burst into tears.

Louisa had moved into the front seat and she put her arms around me.

'I'm sorry,' I sniffed. 'I'm not normally a crier. I'm just shattered. What a morning.'

'Don't be silly,' smiled Louisa. 'It sounds horrendous. I know I would have given up and not taken him. Why do you think he was kicking off?'

I explained what had happened with his parents in the playground the previous day.

'Oh, poor little mite,' sighed Louisa. 'Maybe he was frightened that his mum and stepdad would be there again and this time he would have to go with them?'

'Yes, maybe,' I sighed. 'Or it could be that he wanted to go with them and then they left again?'

Even when children had come from the most dysfunctional and neglectful of homes, it was still their familiar place and they often had a sense of loyalty to their birth parents.

'Well, you got him in and that was enough,' Louisa told me.

'You're right,' I said. 'And hopefully next week will be better.'

I felt much calmer as I drove Louisa back to where she'd left her car.

'Do you want to come back to the flat for a cuppa?' she asked me.

'Thanks but not today, lovey,' I smiled. 'I need to clean my house, which looks like a war zone thanks to Ralph. Thanks again for everything.'

When I got back home, I didn't know what to tackle first – the urine-soaked carpet or the broken mug and vase. I started in the kitchen and got a bucket of soapy water and a sponge to try to get the tea stains off my cream walls.

Then I swept up the pieces of china.

It was only a mug but for some reason, I felt really sad about it. It represented a happy memory of a child finding their forever home with a lovely couple and I'd become really attached to it.

You silly thing, I told myself as I tipped the pieces into the bin.

I could have kicked myself for not putting it out of the way as when you fostered children, things had a habit of getting broken. Over the years, I'd learnt to put anything really precious to me in my bedroom or out of the way in a high cupboard.

I'd just finished clearing up when my phone rang. It was Shelley.

'How were things this morning?' she asked cheerfully.

'It's been a tricky one to say the least,' I told her before filling her in on what had happened.

'Poor Ralph and you,' she sighed. 'It must be so confusing for him.'

She explained that she was ringing to let me know that Renae, Ralph's mum, had finally been in touch.

'She must have finally got one of my letters or messages as she rang me this morning.'

'What did she say?' I asked.

'Well, there was a lot of swearing and asking me in not-so-nice terms to give her her kid back. She referred to you as a b**** and said that you had no right to take Ralph.'

'Charming,' I said.

'I remained very calm and reiterated that Ralph was now in the care of the local authority as her and her partner had left without any trace and had been uncontactable for over a week. I explained that we needed to assess how Ralph had been living and ask her some questions about their home life as well as doing a home visit. I explained that I could arrange for them both to see Ralph as soon as possible but that it would be a supervised contact session at a contact centre.'

'What did she say to that?' I asked.

'She wasn't happy to say the least,' Shelley added. 'There was a lot of swearing about how Ralph was her kid and she didn't need anyone watching her, but I was quite firm with her and said that, at the moment, it was the only way she was going to be able to see her son.

'After that, she hung up.'

After I'd put the phone down to Shelley, I wasn't sure what to think. If Renae and Dean did agree to see Ralph at a contact centre, I just knew it was going to be challenging. I was still deep in my thoughts when my phone rang again. This time it was Vicky.

'Hi, lovey,' I said. 'How are you?'

I suddenly heard a loud sob.

'Oh, Maggie,' she wept. 'I've had some news about the boys. I just can't believe it.'

NINE

No Show

'Oh Vicky,' I sighed. 'What's happened?'

She could hardly get her words out for crying.

'I went to see my solicitor,' she snivelled. 'I got a letter from the LADO today.'

The LADO stood for the Local Authority Designated Officer. When Robert had made his allegations against Vicky, it was the LADO's job to oversee the investigation and to help make a decision about whether an allegation was upheld or not.

'And what did they say?' I asked, my heart in my mouth.

'They decided that that the allegations were unsubstantiated,' said Vicky. 'They're not going to take them any further. I'm in the clear.'

'But that's brilliant news,' I gasped. 'After all this time, you must be so relieved and now you can get the boys back.'

Vicky let out another loud sob.

'I can't get them back Maggie,' she wept. 'It's too late. It's been months since they've lived with me. Nearly eight months to be precise and I haven't been allowed to see them since.

'Talking to their social worker today, they're happy and settled with their new carer,' she continued. 'I can't put them through any more change and upheaval just to make me feel better. I wouldn't do that to them.'

In my opinion, the system was all wrong. Listening to Vicky, sadly I knew that she was right. The boys had been away from her longer than they'd been with her.

I'd seen it happen several times before with other carers. I understood these investigations had to be thorough to protect the children but this had taken months and Vicky had faced so much uncertainty and worry. She'd been put through hell.

'I'm so sorry,' I told her. 'At least your name and your reputation have been cleared and you can carry on fostering now.'

'I just don't know if I can do it anymore,' replied Vicky. 'I'd be living in constant fear that the same thing will happen and another child will make an allegation against me.'

'I don't think I could go through it again.'

I'd never heard Vicky sound so despondent and it broke my heart to hear her say she was considering giving up fostering. But she was right, in fostering circles I was hearing about more and more carers who were facing allegations.

'You're honestly one of the best carers that I know,' I told her. 'You have helped so many children over so many years and it would be such a loss if you gave it all up.'

'I just don't know anymore,' she sighed. 'I've got a lot of thinking to do about my future.'

It was horrible to hear my friend so upset.

'Well, I'm here if you need to talk,' I told her.

'Thanks,' she replied. 'But I know you've got a lot on your plate at the minute. 'I'm not going to rush into any decisions, I need to think this through properly.'

I completely understood.

As the days passed there were thankfully no more appearances from Renae and Dean, and Ralph started to settle back into school.

One afternoon, I picked him up and told him that we were going to see the doctor.

'He's going to check you out to make sure you're all fit and healthy,' I told him cheerfully.

I'd been dreading telling him as I was convinced that he would have a meltdown. However, Ralph looked at me blankly and I'm not sure if he even understood. In fact, he seemed completely disinterested until we got to the GP's surgery.

As we walked into the packed waiting room, I felt him slowing down and pulling back on my hand. Then I remembered the small play area at the back of the surgery.

'Oh look, Ralph, there are some toys over there,' I told him.

I could see he was interested as he led me over to them straight away. I sat on the floor next to him as he rummaged through a wooden toy box, while I kept one ear out for his name to be called.

'Car!' he said, delighted as he dug one out from the bottom.

He played happily with it for the next ten minutes before it was our turn to see the GP.

'Ralph, please can you put the car back?' I asked him. 'The doctor wants to see us now.'

'No!' he said, shaking his head.

I knew it wasn't worth the battle here in front of everyone; the GP was waiting and I didn't want us to miss our appointment, so I had to almost drag him along to the doctor's room.

Dr Henry had only started at the practice six months ago but I'd already taken several of my foster children to see him. It helped having a GP who knew my circumstances so I didn't have to explain each time what my relationship to the child was. He was a newly qualified GP and a lot younger than most of the others at the practice, and I found children really responded well to him and felt comfortable.

'Ralph, this is Dr Henry,' I told him as we walked into his consulting room.

'Hello, Ralph,' he smiled. 'That's a lovely car you've got there. Can I have a look at it?'

Ralph scowled.

'No!' he said, throwing it at him. 'Car mine.'

Dr Henry looked surprised as it bounced off his desk and onto the floor.

'Ralph, we don't throw things,' I told him firmly. 'If you do that, I will take the car away.'

'I'm so sorry about that,' I said to the doctor. 'He's very protective about his cars.'

Ralph had crawled onto the floor to retrieve the car and was now sat under Dr Henry's desk playing.

'Don't worry,' he replied. 'Leave him be while you and I have a chat.'

I could see Ralph was preoccupied with the car so he wasn't tuning into what we were talking about. I explained that he'd only been with me a couple of weeks but that I'd noticed a few things that I wanted to get checked out.

'He's not as verbal as he should be for a six-year-old,' I told him. 'He has massive meltdowns and his behaviour at school and at my house can be very destructive.'

I also described the whooping that he did when he was anxious.

'To me it feels more than just a reaction to coming into the care system or to what was happening at home,' I added. 'Both his teachers and I feel that he needs to be assessed for autism.'

I explained that I'd mentioned it to his teacher and they were going to get an educational psychologist to come and assess Ralph.

'At this point, I don't think there's anything you need to do but I just wanted to pass on the information,' I told him.

'I also wanted to mention something else,' I continued, glancing at Ralph who was still engrossed in his car under the desk.

I explained about his leg

'I've noticed, especially when he runs, that it turns in slightly. It might be nothing and just a habit but I wanted to double-check.'

'Yes, of course,' he replied. 'Let me have a look at it.'

The weather wasn't as warm as it had been of late but I'd deliberately put Ralph in shorts so it would be easier for Dr Henry to examine him.

'Ralph, come over here and show me your car,' I asked him gently.

He peered out from under the table.

'No!' he said.

'Please, Ralph, come and sit here,' I said, patting the examination couch next to me. 'Dr Henry and I would love to see your car.'

'I really would,' Dr Henry nodded encouragingly. 'I promise that I won't touch it.'

Worried that we were going to be there all evening, I put my arms out and picked Ralph up off the floor. Thankfully he didn't struggle.

He was so light, I managed to balance him on my hip.

'Now then, let's get you sat on here,' I said, lowering him gently onto the couch. 'Then you can show us that lovely car.'

But as soon as I put him down, he started to struggle.

'Off! Off!' he yelled.

'You need to stay on here for a minute, Ralph,' I told him. 'Dr Henry needs to have a quick look at your leg.'

Ralph turned to stare at the doctor.

'Good lad,' smiled Dr Henry, putting his hand on Ralph's shoulder. 'I promise you that I'll be very quick and it won't hurt.'

Ralph glared at him and before I could stop him, he lunged forwards and sank his teeth into the doctor's arm.

'Arggh!' yelped Dr Henry, pulling his arm back.

'Ralph!' I gasped. 'We don't bite people!'

'Don't like man,' he shouted, jumping down from the couch and running off. 'No touch me.'

'I'm so sorry,' I told Dr Henry. 'Are you OK?'

I could already see there was a bright red teeth-shaped mark on his arm

'He's broken the skin,' he huffed. 'I'm going to have to have a tetanus jab for that.'

'I really am sorry,' I repeated. 'He's never bitten anyone before.'

The door was closed and the room was small so after running round a few times, Ralph was now cowered back under the desk.

'Look, I'll get an X-ray booked in for you at the hospital,' Dr Henry told me. 'I think that's the only way we can really tell if there's something wrong with his leg or hip. They'll contact you with an appointment.'

'Thank you so much,' I told him. 'And sorry again about the bite.'

He nodded and gave me a polite smile but I could tell that he was keen to get us out of there as quickly as possible.

'Ralph, we're leaving now,' I told him.

This time he needed no encouragement and ran out from under the table and through the door.

A few days later, Shelley got in touch. Ralph had been in my care for over two weeks now and it had been several days since his mum, Renae, had called her.

'Mum finally got back to me and has agreed to contact,' she told me.

Despite how Renae and Dean had behaved when I'd seen them at school, I still thought it was important for Ralph to see his parents. I just hoped they wouldn't be as hostile now that the situation had been explained to them.

'As they were quite volatile when they came to school, I think it needs to be at a secure centre,' Shelley told me, echoing my thoughts.

There were lots of different types of contact centres around the county. Secure ones tended to be used when birth parents had a history of aggressive behaviour or there was a danger of the child being snatched. Unlike ordinary centres, they had security guards on duty and extra security measures in place.

We made a plan for after school in a couple of days' time. I wasn't going to mention it to Ralph until just before we went to the centre as I didn't know how it would affect him and I didn't want him to be anxious or worried.

As I picked him up from school that afternoon, I felt a flicker of nerves. I had no idea how Ralph was going to react to the thought of seeing his parents.

'Ralph, we're not going to go straight back to my house today,' I told him. 'We're going to go to a contact centre where you can play with some toys.'

He looked up at me.

'Cars?' he asked eagerly.

'I'm sure there will be some cars,' I smiled. 'And hopefully we might see Mummy and Daddy there.'

He didn't show any reaction at all to what I'd just told him.

'Sleep at Maggie's?' he asked me, ten minutes later.

I could see that he was trying to process it all in that little brain of his.

'Yes, you're still going to sleep at Maggie's house,' I re-assured him.

Thankfully he seemed to accept that and he was quiet as we drove to the contact centre. It was over on the other side of town and it was a good forty-minute drive away.

'Here we are,' I said cheerfully.

The contact centre was called Chestnut Lodge and it was on the same site as a local authority office. It was in a separate building that looked a bit like a brick bungalow.

'Toys?' asked Ralph as I got him out of this car seat.

'Yes, the toys are in there,' I said, pointing to the building.

As we walked towards the entrance, I noticed a couple of security guards dressed in black uniforms standing outside. To enter, first we had to be buzzed in and then, rather than going straight through to an open reception that led to all of the contact rooms, we were led into an enclosed reception area where there was a receptionist behind a Perspex screen. I showed her my ID and signed us in.

'Shelley should be expecting us,' I told her.

Finally we were buzzed through some more security doors to where the contact rooms were. As we walked through, there were another couple of burly security guards standing around. They didn't say anything but you were certainly aware of their presence.

Shelley was sat in the waiting area doing some work. She got up when she saw us.

'Hello, Ralph,' she smiled. 'Did you have a good day at school?'

'Toys?' he repeated to her.

'Yes, I can show you where the toys are,' she told him.

'I've told him there will be lots of toys for him to play with,' I added.

Shelley went over to one of the contact rooms and unlocked the door. It was the usual set up – a faded sofa and some chairs like the ones you'd find in a doctor's waiting room, a scratched coffee table and a worn striped rug. A few tired-looking boxes of toys and a shelf full of old books lined the walls. Some contact rooms had doors that opened out to a small garden or a kitchen but this was just a secure, enclosed space.

'Let's see if we can find you some cars,' I told Ralph.

I knelt down on the rug and rummaged through one of the

toy boxes. Eventually I fished out a few tatty-looking Matchbox cars. Ralph's face lit up and he grabbed them eagerly.

It was enough to keep him occupied while Shelley and I sat in the corner and had a quiet chat out of his earshot.

'Any sign of Renae and Dean?' I asked her.

'Not yet,' she shrugged. 'But I did tell them to be here fifteen minutes after you as I didn't want to risk you bumping into them outside.'

She explained that, at the end of the session, Ralph and I would leave first, then she'd stay with the parents and they wouldn't leave until fifteen minutes after us.

'I've asked reception to let me know as soon as they arrive so you can go into one of the offices before they buzz them through,' she told me. 'I just thought it would be better for you to be out of the way in case they get aggressive again.'

'Absolutely,' I nodded. 'That's fine by me.'

I was happy to keep out of sight if it meant that I could avoid a torrent of abuse and I didn't want Ralph to have to witness that. I'd brought some paperwork to be getting on with during the hour-long session.

'How did Ralph react to you telling him that he was coming here?' Shelley asked me.

'I don't think he fully understands,' I said. 'As far as he's concerned, he's just playing with some toys in a room. I don't think it will fully hit home that his parents are coming until he sees them.'

'Maybe that's a good thing,' she shrugged.

Shelley looked up at the clock.

'They should be here by now,' she tutted.

Parents were always given a fifteen-minute grace period in

case there was a genuine delay. But after that time the session would automatically be cancelled. It was designed that way so children didn't have to spend ages hanging around and waiting.

'Hopefully now they know what's happening, they'll be a lot calmer today,' said Shelley hopefully. 'And if they're not, then there are measures in place.'

I'd already noticed the discreet button on the wall near the sofa. If there was any sense of trouble or they were worried about the safety of the children or themselves, staff could press the button and the security guards would be in there in seconds.

Time ticked on. Five minutes late turned to ten minutes and there was still no sign of Renae or Dean.

'I'll just nip out and give them a quick call,' Shelley told me.

Thankfully Ralph was still transfixed by the cars and was running them up and down the back of the sofa.

Shelley came back in a few seconds later.

'I can't get through,' she shrugged.

As the clock ticked and fifteen minutes turned to twenty, we caught each other's eye.

'I think we need to call it a day,' nodded Shelley. 'I don't want Ralph to have to hang round any longer.'

I always felt a heavy sense of sadness when a birth parent failed to turn up for contact. This was a chance to see their child, who had been taken into care, for the first time in weeks and they couldn't even be bothered to turn up.

'There might be a genuine reason,' sighed Shelley.

But I think we both knew deep down inside that that probably wasn't the case. If there was, they could have called the contact centre or Shelley, or picked up when she'd rung them.

I just felt desperately sad for Ralph although thankfully he still seemed to be oblivious as to why we were there.

'You're going back to Maggie's house now,' Shelley told him.

'Toys?' he asked.

'The toys are staying here but hopefully you'll come back and play with them again another time,' I said.

'Sleep at Maggie's house?' he asked.

'Yes, you're going back to Maggie's now,' nodded Shelley. 'Hopefully Mummy and Daddy will come another time.'

Birth parents had a right to see their children and the courts always frowned on Social Services if they didn't try to give them the opportunity. Renae and Dean would be given other chances to see Ralph so I knew we'd have to go through this all again.

The security guards walked us out to the car park just in case Ralph's parents suddenly did turn up.

As we drove home, Ralph was quiet in the back. It was always heartbreaking for children when their parents didn't turn up for contact. I'd put children in a taxi with a contact worker and they'd returned half an hour later in utter distress because Mummy and Daddy hadn't come. But with Ralph, I didn't know what on earth he was thinking.

Shelley called me as soon as we got back.

'I've just got hold of Renae and Dean,' she told me. 'They said they had to go and sort out their benefit and then the bus was cancelled. We've agreed that we'll reschedule the session in a couple of days,' she said.

Would next time be any different? I knew Ralph's parents had the legal right to see him but the fear and distress he showed around them was so upsetting. For Ralph's sake, I hated having to put him through that again.

TEN

Rages and Revelations

Holding tightly onto Ralph's hand, we walked across the car park.

'Here we are again,' I smiled.

It was four days later and we were back at Chestnut House for another contact session. This time I really hoped that things would be different and that Renae and Dean were going to turn up.

'Can you remember the contact centre from the other day?' I asked him. 'Shelley will be waiting for us inside and Mummy and Daddy might come and see you.'

After last time, I was hesitant to mention Mummy or Daddy but I wanted Ralph to be prepared. But my emphasis was very much on the 'might'.

'Toys?' asked Ralph.

'Yes, there are going to be toys,' I smiled. 'Remember there was a big toy box there?'

After the other day, we knew where we were going this time. We were quickly buzzed through both sets of security doors and into the reception area where Shelley was waiting. The door to one of the contact rooms was already open and, before I could stop him, Ralph ran in and sat himself down on the floor next to the toy box.

'Someone's making himself at home,' smiled Shelley.

'That's good,' I nodded.

I didn't want the contact centre to become a place that Ralph dreaded going to. Some children that I'd fostered in the past would start crying even before they'd gone in because they recognised the building and knew that it meant seeing their birth parents. Others would become absolutely hyper and start playing up the moment they saw the contact centre. Contact could be an overwhelming or stressful experience for little ones and they all reacted to it in different ways.

Shelley made us both a coffee and we went to sit with Ralph while he played. He'd emptied the toy box out onto the rug and was engrossed in examining each toy.

'Do you think they'll show up this time?' I asked her quietly.

'I rang and spoke to Renae this morning and she assured me that they will be here,' she shrugged.

She'd advised Renae on bus routes and looked up the timetable for them. I knew Social Services had to offer birth parents the opportunity to see their child, even when it was a child who had suffered appalling neglect and cruelty at their hands. But from my personal perspective, I hoped that they would back out at the last minute and not turn up. I just didn't want Ralph to be put through it all again.

Shelley introduced me to the contact worker, Katie, who was also going to be in the room as she'd be supervising the sessions going forward. As it was the first one, Shelley wanted to be there too. As we chatted, I couldn't help but be conscious of the time and have one eye on the clock.

Ten minutes later, the receptionist came into the room.

'Just to let you know the parents are here and they've been buzzed into the waiting area,' she told Shelley.

'Great,' Shelley replied. 'I'll give you a shout when it's OK to let them through.'

I wanted to make sure I was well out of the way by the time they came in as I didn't want Renae and Dean to see me in case it antagonised them.

'Ralph, I'm going to go and drink my coffee in another room,' I told him casually.

As he looked up at me, I could see the panic in his eyes.

'No!' he shouted. 'No!'

'It's OK, Ralph,' Shelley soothed. 'Katie and I are staying here with you, and Maggie will come back once she's had her coffee.'

'I won't be long,' I added.

'No!' he repeated.

'Ooh, Ralph, have you seen this garage?' Katie asked, trying her best to distract him. 'Can your cars go down the ramp?'

I quickly left the room. I wanted Ralph to be calm and a bit more settled by the time his parents came in.

I went into a little office off the main reception area that Shelley had told me would be free. I shut the door and got out some paperwork to try to take my mind off what was going on in the contact room. The next thing I knew, I heard the buzz of the security doors opening and Renae and Dean came clattering into reception. I couldn't help but peep through the glass panels in the door.

They looked as dishevelled as they'd been when I saw them in the school playground. Even though it was a mild afternoon, Renae was wearing a tatty black winter coat with the hood up and Dean was in dirty jeans and a T-shirt. He kept scratching his arms and he looked fidgety and on edge.

Shelley came out to see them and they had a conversation. After a few minutes, I could tell that all wasn't well as I could hear their raised voices through the glass.

'Don't you be f***ing telling us what to do,' I heard Dean shout. 'I told you we ain't been drinking or taking nothing. Now let us see the lad.'

'What sort of b**** stops someone from seeing their kid?' spat Renae.

I could tell from her facial expressions that Shelley was doing her best to try to calm them down.

'Your son is in there listening and if you want to see him then you need to tone it down, otherwise this contact session will not be happening,' she told them firmly. 'Aggressive behaviour will not be tolerated.'

They carried on shouting and swearing and then they started arguing between themselves. Renae shouted and screamed at Dean and he kicked a bin and sent it flying across the floor. Suddenly two security guards appeared and one of them stood between the couple and the other went over to Dean.

'Don't f***ing touch me,' he spat.

'I'm afraid I can't allow this contact session to happen today,' Shelley told them. 'It's clear to me that you're both under the influence of something and we can't put up with aggressive behaviour like this.'

Dean started kicking off again.

'The social can't stop us from seeing our lad,' he yelled. 'You're all f***ing child snatchers!'

The security guard restrained him and he was quickly buzzed out of the reception area and into the holding zone. He was swiftly followed by Renae who was still hurling abuse at Shelley as she was marched out by another security guard.

I was about to breathe a sigh of relief that they'd gone but there was suddenly a loud thumping on the security door and I could see Dean's angry face pressed up against the glass out in the waiting area.

'You're gonna f***ing regret this!' he yelled before the security guard quickly pulled him away.

I left it a few minutes and, once I was sure that they'd gone, I opened the office door and came out into reception. Shelley looked pretty shaken.

'Are you OK?' I asked her. 'That sounded like it was getting pretty nasty.'

'They were as high as kites,' she sighed. 'Their pupils were massive and they stank of alcohol. There's no way I could let them see Ralph like that.'

Just as she'd said that, there was an almighty crash followed by the sound of breaking glass.

'Ralph, no!' I heard Katie, the contact worker shout.

Shelley and I ran into the contact room to be met with a scene of absolute devastation. The window was smashed and the carpet was covered in shards of broken glass. There were toys and cushions all over the floor, books had been ripped, the coffee table was on its side.

'What the heck has happened here?' gasped Shelley.

I knew instantly.

Ralph.

'As soon as he heard his parents' voices, he got very distressed and started to have a meltdown,' sighed Katie. 'He was running around and throwing things and he was making a funny noise. I'm sorry, I tried to stop him but I couldn't.'

'What happened to the window?' asked Shelley.

'He threw a mug at it and it just shattered,' she replied.

I think smashing the window had given Ralph a shock and, for once, he was sitting quietly on the rug, staring at the mess all around him. The security guards must have heard the commotion too as they came running into the room.

'It's OK,' Shelley told them. 'We've got this covered.'

'We thought the dad had found his way round the back and made another appearance,' one of the guards told her.

'Actually, would you mind going outside and double-checking that they've left the premises?' she asked him. 'I don't want to take any chances.'

Ralph was still sitting on the floor.

'Come and sit on the sofa with me,' I told him.

For once, he did as I'd asked. He was quiet and his eyes were glazed, almost like he was in a trance. I took hold of his hands but he didn't make eye contact with me.

'Ralph, we don't smash windows,' I said firmly. 'It's so dangerous. You could have hurt yourself or someone else.'

I paused.

'Did you hear Mummy and Daddy shouting?' I asked him.

He glanced up at me with a confused look.

'Sleep at Maggie's?' he asked.

'Yes, you're going to sleep at Maggie's house tonight,' I said.

That seemed to have become Ralph's way of seeking assurance from me.

I sat there holding his hands as Katie and Shelley started clearing up the glass around us. He looked totally and utterly bewildered.

Before we left, Shelley and I had a quick chat outside.

'I'm going to take him back now,' I told her.

'I can't believe a six-year-old can be so destructive,' she replied. 'Perhaps he heard his mum and dad and that was his way of showing his upset at not seeing them?'

I didn't share Shelley's opinion.

'In my opinion, Ralph's not showing frustration and anger that he hasn't seen his parents,' I told her. 'It's fear that he's about to.'

'What will happen now?' I asked.

'I'll go and visit Renae and Dean and explain again the kind of behaviour that won't be tolerated at contact,' she added. 'Then, next time, I will get them here before you and Ralph so I can make sure they are in a fit state to see him and avoid what happened today.'

My heart sank.

'You know we have to keep offering them the opportunity to have contact with their child,' Shelley told me. 'Any judge would frown on us not offering them that.'

'I know,' I replied. 'It doesn't make it any easier for Ralph though.'

'I think we'll leave it until next week to schedule another session after what happened today. It's a lot for a child as young as Ralph to cope with,' she added.

'That's a good idea,' I agreed.

To be honest, it was a lot for all of us.

I went back into the contact room. Ralph was still sitting on the sofa, spinning the wheels of a toy car. He looked exhausted.

'We're going to go back now,' I told him.

He jumped up eagerly.

'I'll get one of the security guards to walk you back to your car just in case,' Shelley told me.

'Thanks,' I replied.

There was no harm in being extra-vigilant. As we walked across the car park, I noticed Ralph was still clutching the car from the contact centre.

'We'll have to bring that back another day,' I told him.

By the time we got home, I was exhausted too. It was an adrenalin rush for everyone involved when that kind of situation happens at a contact session. It felt so nice to see Amena, and I made sure I stuck to the usual routine of dinner, bath and bed to keep things quiet and consistent for Ralph.

He hardly said a word for the rest of the night.

'What's wrong with him?' Amena asked suspiciously.

'He's had a long day and I think he's very tired,' I replied.

He got into the bath without any objections and I could see that he was soothed by the warm water.

'Did you enjoy your pasta that you had for tea?' I asked him as I gently washed him down.

'Pasta,' he nodded. 'Sausages?'

'Yes,' I told him. 'We're going to have sausages for tea tomorrow as I know they're your favourite.'

I pulled the plug out of the bath and was just about to stand Ralph up and wrap a bath towel around him when he turned to me.

'Daddy shout,' he said.

'Did you hear Daddy shouting at the contact centre?' I asked him and he nodded.

I waited to see whether Ralph would say anything else but he didn't and I didn't want to push him to talk about it.

'We're going to do your teeth now and then we'll have a story and then you're going to sleep at Maggie's,' I told him.

All I could do was stick to the routine and keep things consistent for him and hopefully that would help Ralph to feel safe and secure.

Early the following week, Ralph had an appointment for his leg to be X-rayed at the local hospital after Dr Henry had referred us. After how he had reacted at the GP surgery, I was dreading it.

I'd already been in touch with the hospital and explained that I was fostering Ralph and I suspected that he had additional needs and might struggle to cope with being X-rayed. They had very kindly sent me a special pictural guide for him and I to read together, explaining the process so that he would know exactly what to expect.

A couple of days before his appointment, I went through it with him. Each page was simply set out with big writing and lots of pictures showing what would happen throughout the whole appointment.

I will go to reception, said the first page with a photo of the actual reception desk. *I will go to the waiting area and a radiographer will call my name*, said the second page.

I read it to Ralph and showed him the photographs. It prepared him for the fact that someone would be moving him around and he'd have to keep still and machines would be beeping. He seemed to be taking it all in.

'An X-ray is a special picture that the doctors take of you,' I explained. 'It's a bit like a photograph and it shows them what's going on inside your leg. We need to go to the hospital to have it done and they'll take us into a special room where there will be a big camera hanging from the ceiling.'

'Hospital,' Ralph repeated and I nodded.

'You can take your favourite car with you,' I told him.

However, despite all the preparation, I wasn't sure how Ralph was going to react. I knew it was going to be a lot for him to cope with so Shelley had agreed that he could have the day off school.

On the morning of his appointment, I went through the book with him again. Thankfully Ralph seemed calm and a little curious as we walked through the hospital and I gave him a running commentary on what we were doing.

'Hospitals are very busy places,' I said. 'There are lots of people here and did you see the ambulances outside?'

I knew he was fascinated by any sort of vehicle.

'Oh look, here's the reception area just like we saw in your book,' I told him.

Thankfully we didn't have to wait long until his name was called and we walked into the X-ray room.

'Hello, Ralph,' said a smiley dark-haired lady. 'I'm Sue and I'm going to be taking a picture of your leg today. And this is Jess, who's going to be helping me out.'

Jess smiled. She looked a lot younger and I guessed she was a student.

'Look, Ralph, the room is dark just like your book said it would be,' I told him.

'Ah, you've been reading the special book,' smiled Sue. 'You'll know exactly what's going to happen then. We'll need you to lie down on the bed first. You've got your baggy shorts on so we won't need to take those off. Well done Mum for remembering,' she added.

'Actually, I'm his foster carer,' I said, correcting her.

'I'm so sorry,' she replied. 'I think I had read that on the notes.'

We had a quiet chat to one side and I explained that I was worried that Ralph would be distressed and wouldn't manage to keep still.

'Would you mind if I showed him what he needs to do?' I asked her.

'If you think that would help him then that's fine,' she replied.

I lay down on the bed to show him that it wasn't scary.

'Look, Ralph,' I smiled. 'You need to do this and then keep very, very still while the special X-ray machine takes a picture of your leg. Remember what the book said?' I added. 'There will be a loud beep and that means it's taking the picture. It doesn't hurt at all and then afterwards you can have your car.'

Ralph nodded.

'Would it be OK if I try to get him into the right position myself as I'm worried that he'll get freaked out by strangers touching him?'

I remembered how he'd reacted to Dr Henry and I didn't want to take that chance.

'We can certainly give it a try,' smiled Sue. 'And remember, Ralph, sometimes we might move the bed around too so it might feel like you're on a train.'

'Train,' repeated Ralph.

Much to my relief, he seemed fascinated rather than frightened by what was happening.

Ralph got on the bed OK and Sue handed me a lead apron to wear to minimise any radiation. She guided me through what positions he needed to be in.

'I'm going to move this big camera now so it can take a photo but it won't touch you and I promise you that it's not going to hurt.'

Sue and Jess moved to the other side of the room and stood behind a counter while I held Ralph's leg in the correct position.

'Ralph, they're going to take the picture of your leg now and you've got to stay really, really still so they get a clear picture otherwise they'll have to do it all over again,' I told him.

He looked up at me and nodded.

'Good boy, Ralph,' Sue told him. 'You're doing really well. Now you're going to see the camera light shine on your body and it will make a clicking sound then there will be a loud beep.'

Ralph looked nervous and I held my breath as Jess pressed the button on the machine, but amazingly, he managed to keep still.

'Well done, Ralph,' smiled Sue. 'You're doing great. We just need to take a few more pictures. I want to make sure we get both the upper and lower leg and the hip,' she told Jess.

Jess moved the camera and the bed so they could get a different angle. Ralph started to get a bit wriggly.

'Stay nice and still, Ralph,' Sue told him. 'Just like you're playing musical statues.'

Thankfully Ralph did as she asked.

'All done,' she smiled after ten minutes. 'What a great job, Ralph. You can get down now.'

'Well done,' I told him. 'You did so, so well.'

'Car,' he asked me straight away

'Yes,' I smiled. 'You can have your car.'

To be honest, I'd been expecting the worst and it was such a relief that he hadn't become distressed or had a meltdown. While Ralph played with his car on the floor, I went over to their counter where they had the images up on a computer.

'How does it look?' I asked her. 'I know it needs to be looked at by a doctor but can you see if there's anything obviously wrong with his leg?'

Both Sue and Jess were staring at the screen and talking in a low voice.

'If you could wait here for a minute that would be great,' Sue told me. 'I'm just going to go and find a doctor.'

Then she left the room.

It struck me as odd as I'd been told we'd have to come back another time to speak to a doctor as they didn't look at the images right away.

'Is everything OK?' I asked Jess.

She looked very awkward.

'I-I'm not sure,' she stuttered. 'Sue has gone to speak to the doctor.'

I could tell by the way she was acting that something wasn't right.

Ten minutes later, Sue came back in the room. I was puzzled

when I saw a man in a suit with her and a security guard.

'What's going on?' I asked.

The man introduced himself as a consultant radiologist but I didn't catch his name.

'I need you to come with me please so we can have a chat in my office,' he said.

'OK,' I replied. 'Can I bring Ralph with me?'

'I'm afraid not,' said the consultant. 'You need to come on your own.'

There was something about his manner that chilled me to the bone and told me that something was very wrong.

ELEVEN

Horror at the Hospital

As I was taken into an office, all I could think about was Ralph's little face and the fearful look in his eyes as I had been led away.

There was a woman already in there.

'I'm Dr Brown, a consultant radiologist,' the man explained again as he sat down behind a desk. 'And this is Miriam Kratz, who is part of the trust's safeguarding team.'

'What's this about?' I asked them. 'Ralph looked absolutely terrified to see me being marched out like that.'

Dr Brown cleared his throat.

'Ralph's X-ray has shown up multiple fractures of his left leg,' he told me. 'There's a transverse fracture of the femur, a hip fracture . . .'

As he continued, I switched off. My head was spinning and I couldn't believe what I was hearing.

'How has he done that?' I asked.

'We're not sure,' shrugged Dr Brown. 'What we do know is that the fractures are all at different stages of healing.'

'What does that mean?' I asked, even more confused.

'It signifies that the injuries happened at different times – they didn't all happen at once from one single incident,' he explained.

'Has Ralph hurt himself or been in an accident that you can recall?' he asked while Miriam Kratz took notes.

'No,' I said, shaking my head. 'Not while I've been fostering him, but he's only been with me for a month.'

Dr Brown and Miriam exchanged glances.

'Look, please can you contact Ralph's social worker,' I told them. 'I feel like you need to speak to both of us about this. I can assure you that he hasn't suffered these fractures while he's been in my care and prior to that he was with his birth mother. Can you not see when he was treated from his hospital records?' I added.

'There are no hospital records anywhere in the country for Ralph that we can find, so we can only assume that he never had treatment and that the fractures have just been left to heal on their own,' replied Dr Brown.

My heart broke for Ralph. He must have been in so much pain. *Poor little lad.*

I gave them Shelley's name and number and they said they would contact her straight away.

'What happens now?' I asked them.

'If you could wait in here for the time being and we'll come and update you when I've had time to chat to Dr Brown and my colleagues,' Miriam told me.

They both got up and left.

I knew I needed to call Becky and let her know what was happening.

'Oh, Maggie,' she sighed. 'That sounds awful. Poor Ralph.'

'I know,' I replied. 'It's so upsetting thinking he had all these fractures but nobody took him to the hospital.

'I think I was in shock when the doctor was talking to me and I couldn't take it all in,' I added. 'I feel as if I'm under suspicion, even though from the way the doctor was talking, it seems as if these injuries are months old.'

'Maggie, I'm going to call Shelley now myself and ask her to come up to the hospital straight away to see you,' Becky told me. 'But ring me if you need anything else. I'm so sorry this has happened.'

I could hear the concern in her voice.

'Thank you,' I sighed. 'So am I.'

As I sat there, alone in the consultant's office, so many thoughts were swirling around my head. Surely the doctors didn't suspect that I'd hurt Ralph? They knew his injuries happened several months ago, didn't they?

The only logical explanation to me was that they had happened when he was with his parents. I knew the police would need to be involved now. Would Dean and Renae be arrested? Would Ralph have to be interviewed? I had so many questions.

Half an hour later, Shelley walked into the office.

'Oh, I'm so pleased to see you,' I said, rushing up to her. 'They're saying Ralph's got multiple fractures and I feel like I'm the one under suspicion. They marched me away from him and I haven't seen him since.'

'Maggie, it's OK,' Shelley told me. 'Ralph's fine. I've just seen him and he's playing with some toys in a playroom on the paediatric ward.'

'Oh, thank goodness,' I sighed, feeling relief wash over me.

Shelley explained that she'd just spoken to the doctor and the safeguarding team.

'You're not under suspicion,' she told me. 'They can estimate the time frame of the fractures and they can see they're all several months old. They pre-date you having Ralph so they must have happened when he was living with his birth mother and stepfather.'

'Poor little thing,' I sighed, feeling both relief that the doctors knew it wasn't me and deep shock at what Ralph had been through.

'We don't have a full picture yet,' Shelley told me. 'At the moment, they're being treated as multiple, unexplained fractures but for all we know, there might be a reasonable explanation for them. We have to keep an open mind until we speak to Renae and Dean.'

'The way the doctor was talking, he seemed to believe they were old injuries that have just been left to heal,' I replied.

'That might be the case,' shrugged Shelley. 'But more questions need to be asked.'

She explained that the doctors wanted to do more tests on Ralph.

'They want to do what they call a skeletal survey so they can X-ray all of the bones in his body and see if he has any other injuries,' she told me. 'Depending on the results of that, they might also want to do a CT scan or an MRI.'

They also wanted to do blood tests and tests to check that Ralph didn't have rickets or any other bone disorders that meant he was susceptible to fractures.

'Will he have to stay in overnight?' I asked.

'It depends,' she shrugged. 'They're hoping to get it all done today but you know how long these things can take at the best of times.'

I made a mental note to call Louisa and ask her to look after Amena for me. She'd be coming home to an empty house and wouldn't know where we were.

'Are you going to get the police involved?' I asked Shelley.

'The hospital safeguarding team have already informed them as is their policy,' she told me. 'Officers are on their way up so they'll want to speak to the doctors and probably to you and me.'

'Do you think they'll arrest Renae and Dean?' I asked.

'Renae and Dean aren't due to see Ralph for another few days so I think the police will want to wait until they know what the scans and tests show. They'll probably want to speak to Mrs White and the school too, try to and get a fuller picture before they bring them in for any sort of questioning.'

'Will they want to speak to Ralph?' I added.

'I honestly don't know,' Shelley replied.

Just then, Dr Brown came back in and asked if we wanted to go and see Ralph.

'I need to give Louisa a quick call first,' I told Shelley.

Louisa was part of my carer support package. That meant if I ever needed help or cover with any of my foster placements, Louisa had had the relevant checks, assessments and training that meant that she could step in. She could look after my foster children in the day and have them overnight at my house or at her flat if necessary. As a single carer, it was crucial that I had a good support network, especially for times like this when unexpected things happened.

I quickly phoned Louisa.

'I'm at the hospital with Ralph as he was having some X-rays done,' I told her. 'A few things have come up and the doctors want to keep him in and do more tests.'

'Oh, I'm sorry to hear that,' she replied.

'I'm hoping they'll let us go home later but just in case we don't, please could you have Amena overnight?'

Even though she was sixteen, it didn't feel right leaving her home alone by herself for hours after school and definitely not overnight. I knew how long these things could take so I wanted to be prepared.

'Of course I can,' Louisa told me. 'I'll pop into your house on the way back from work and let her know what's happening.'

'Thanks, lovey,' I told her. 'I'll try to ring her after school and I'll keep you in the loop.'

At least it was one less thing to worry about.

I walked out of the office and into the corridor where Dr Brown and Shelley were waiting.

'We've found Ralph a bed on a paediatric ward so a nurse has taken him down there,' Dr Brown explained.

I was worried that Ralph would be having a complete meltdown by now, being in an unfamiliar place with unfamiliar people but, to my surprise, he was sitting on the bed playing with some cars.

I felt my eyes filling with tears when I saw him, thinking about all the pain he must have been in and him not having the words to tell anyone.

'I see you've found the cars, Ralph,' I smiled, swallowing the lump in my throat.

'He has,' replied the nurse. 'We went on a hunt for cars didn't we, Ralph? I told you we'd find some.'

'I hear you've been a really brave boy, Ralph, while the doctors looked at your leg,' Shelley told him.

He didn't respond to any of us. He was too engrossed in the cars.

The nurse drew the curtains around Ralph's bed and we stepped outside.

'We're going to take some blood in a little while and then later this afternoon we're going to take him for a skeletal survey.'

I explained my worries about Ralph staying still for that long and how he was prone to meltdowns.

'Amazingly he was OK with the X-rays but they were fairly quick,' I told her.

'I've already had a chat with the doctor and we've decided the best thing will be to sedate him as it takes quite a while and we have to move him into different positions to make sure we get clear enough pictures,' she explained.

'That sounds like a good idea,' I replied.

It was a huge relief.

But he had to get through the blood tests first.

'My colleague and I have got a technique that tends to work with most little ones,' she said.

Back in the cubicle, she wheeled a little TV on a stand over to Ralph's bed and moved the screen so he could see it.

'I was going to put on some cartoons but I know just the thing for you,' she smiled.

Luckily there was a programme on about Formula One racing and Ralph was transfixed. He was so busy staring up at the screen that he didn't even flinch when the nurse and her colleague took several vials of blood.

'Do you have to put a needle in his arm to give him the sedation too?' I asked her.

'No, it's a liquid he needs to swallow rather than a cannula,' the nurse explained.

She explained that he couldn't have it until later as he wasn't allowed to eat for six hours beforehand. He'd had breakfast so it would be early afternoon before he could be sedated and taken down for his scan.

The rest of the day was spent waiting around. It was hard as I could tell Ralph was hungry but I managed to distract him with toys. It meant that he was eager to drink the liquid when the nurse gave it to him though.

Then it was more waiting for me until he came back from his scan. I went for a walk around the hospital and grabbed a cup of molten hot tea from a vending machine. By the time I returned to the ward, Ralph was being wheeled back.

'He was an absolute angel,' smiled the nurse.

I could tell he was still really groggy.

'He might feel a bit sick or woozy but we'll bring him some toast in a little while,' she told me.

I could see the sedation had made Ralph tired and sleepy but he wolfed down the toast and jam when it came. It was 6 p.m. now.

'What happens now?' I asked the nurse.

'You'll need to wait around until the doctor has looked at the scan and the blood test results,' she replied.

It was another couple of hours before Dr Brown came to see us. By then, Ralph had dozed off.

'Sorry for the wait,' he said. 'It's been a busy day. How's Ralph doing?'

'He's been really calm,' I replied. 'But I can see he's shattered now.'

He explained that he'd gone through Ralph's scans and test results.

'As well as the hip and leg fractures, I'm afraid we also found that Ralph has several rib fractures,' he told me.

My heart sank.

'Like his other injuries, they're at different stages of healing so that tells us they were not all done at the same time.'

'How might he have fractured his ribs?' I asked.

Dr Brown shrugged.

'Unlike leg or arm fractures, rib fractures are not the kind of injuries that tend to happen day-to-day in a child's life,' he told me. 'A considerable amount of force is needed to cause that kind of trauma so we only expect to see them if a child has been involved in a car crash, for example.'

He paused.

I felt sick as I could see where this was going.

'I'm afraid these type of fractures tend to be highly indicative of child abuse.'

As his words sunk in, my heart broke for Ralph. The only logical explanation was that he'd suffered these injuries at the hands of his birth mum or her partner. I hated to think of him alone and in pain, probably not having the words to tell anyone what had happened.

'I'll pass all of this information on to Ralph's social worker and the police, as is our safeguarding procedure,' he told me.

'Will Ralph have to stay in overnight?' I asked.

'No,' Dr Brown said. 'You can take him home whenever you like.'

Ralph was still sleeping and even though I was reluctant to wake him, I knew he'd be more comfortable in his bedroom at my house. The nurse kindly got me a wheelchair so I could wheel him out to the car.

He was still really groggy when I woke him up.

'Come on, flower, let's get you in your clothes and I'll take you back to Maggie's house,' I said as I undid the hospital gown.

I was always very careful not to refer to my house as 'home' to foster children.

It was nearly 10 p.m. by the time we pulled up outside. The house was in darkness as I carried Ralph through the front door. Amena was at Louisa's and was going to go straight to school from there in the morning.

Ralph was exhausted and still slightly woozy from the sedation so I took him upstairs and put him straight to bed. I took off his socks and shoes and didn't even attempt to get him into his pyjamas.

I watched as he murmured in his sleep and then curled up on his side. He looked so small and frail.

When I came downstairs into the kitchen, I noticed that Louisa had left a note on the side.

Hope all OK and Ralph got discharged. There are two portions of lasagne in the fridge if you're hungry when you get back from the hospital xx.

'You absolute angel,' I sighed to myself.

It was only after I'd read Louisa's note that I realised I was starving. After everything that had happened at the hospital today, I hadn't managed to eat anything other than a packet of crisps that Shelley had got me from a vending machine.

I was shattered but I wanted to call Becky to update her.

'Sorry to ring so late but I just wanted to let you know that we're home,' I told her.

'I'm so glad you didn't have to stay in,' she replied.

I told her what the doctor had said.

'Oh, Maggie,' she sighed. 'That's horrific. Poor little mite.'

'Obviously we don't yet know for sure how he got his fractures but I suppose the police and Social Services will have to investigate now.'

'Well, try and get some sleep and we'll catch up in the morning,' Becky said.

As I put the phone down, my heart felt heavy imagining what Ralph might have been through. The thought of someone hurting him made me want to be physically sick.

'It's OK, Ralph,' I said out loud. 'I promise you that you're safe now.'

There and then I made a vow – no one was ever going to be allowed to hurt him again.

TWELVE

School Shock

My head felt thick and groggy as I forced my eyes open and looked at the clock. I could tell I'd had one of those deep sleeps where you wake up completely confused, not knowing what day it was.

9 a.m.

I went into panic mode and jumped out of bed before the events of the previous day suddenly came flooding back to me. I sank back down under the duvet and sighed.

Poor Ralph.

He must still be asleep, which was good as the nurses had warned me that the sedation would leave him feeling very tired for a day or two. I was still struggling to get my head around what he had been through.

I knew it was dangerous to make assumptions but I couldn't imagine there was a reasonable explanation for all of the fractures that had shown up on his scans. I knew children of Ralph's age were always on the go and they could injure themselves by playing roughly or having an accident.

However, it was the fractured ribs that had really made the medical staff and me suspicious, especially as they had clearly happened at different times. It seemed too far-fetched to think that Ralph had been in two car crashes or had had two incidents that had subjected him to the extreme force needed to do that much damage to his little body.

It was already heartbreaking to know that he'd clearly suffered neglect and had had to live in squalor, but to learn that he might have suffered physical abuse as well was just unthinkable. He'd obviously got used to living in pain, which was an horrific thing for any child.

After a minute or two, I dragged myself out of bed and pulled on my dressing gown. I knew both Ralph and I needed a slow, quiet morning. Even though I'd spent most of the previous day sitting around at the hospital, I felt shattered.

I knew there was also a list of people that I had to contact. Amena had gone straight to school from Louisa's flat this morning and I wanted to ring Louisa and check that everything was OK. I needed to call Ralph's school and let them know that he wouldn't be in again today and, most importantly, I needed to speak to Shelley and find out what was going to happen now.

I tiptoed down the landing and peeped my head around Ralph's door. I could see that he was still curled up in bed, fast asleep.

I went downstairs and sat at the kitchen table with a cup of tea. It was early October and I could see the trees were now in full autumn colour and that the garden was under a thin carpet of leaves.

I spoke to school first. I knew Shelley would be getting in touch with Miss Loughran to fill her in on what had happened but I explained to the school secretary that Ralph had been in hospital until late last night and was still asleep so he wouldn't be in. Then I had a quick chat to Louisa.

'Thanks for the lasagne,' I told her. 'That was exactly what I needed at the end of a long day.'

'I thought it might be,' she replied.

She said that Amena had been fine.

'She played with Edie and helped me put her to bed, then me, her and Charlie watched a film,' she told me. 'She's such a sweet girl.'

'That's good,' I nodded. 'I bet she had a great time.'

My final call was to Shelley.

'How's Ralph doing after yesterday?' she asked.

'He was shattered last night after the sedation and he's still fast asleep now,' I told her.

'He's really been through it,' she sighed.

'So what's going to happen now?' I asked her.

Shelley explained that, after what the scans had revealed, she had organised a child protection case conference to be held at Social Services that afternoon. It was a meeting of all the professionals involved with Ralph, including Miss Loughran and someone from the police. They would have all of Ralph's medical reports from the hospital and would discuss what was going to happen moving forward. I wasn't able to attend as foster carers weren't considered professionals, something that had always annoyed and frustrated me in equal measure.

'I'll call you this afternoon and let you know how it went and what's been decided,' Shelley told me.

'Thank you,' I said.

After I'd put down the phone to her, I could hear the sounds of Ralph stirring upstairs. When I went up to see him, he was standing in his bedroom doorway.

'Morning, Ralph,' I smiled. 'You've had a lovely long sleep. Would you like some breakfast?'

'Sausages,' he nodded.

His blue eyes were sunk back into his head and I could tell he was still groggy from the sedation, which made him much quieter and more amenable than usual. After breakfast, he was happy to lie on the sofa with a duvet, his favourite cars clutched in his hands, while watching cartoons.

I wasn't going to talk to him about what had happened at the hospital or his parents unless he brought it up himself. I had to be really mindful of any impending police investigation and I didn't want there to be any accusations that I had influenced him in any way.

Just after 4 p.m., Amena arrived back from school.

'Hi, flower,' I smiled. 'I'm sorry about yesterday but we got held up at the hospital.'

'Is Ralph OK?' she asked.

She hadn't particularly warmed to him but I could see the genuine concern in her eyes.

'He's absolutely fine, don't you worry,' I replied. 'He just needed a few extra tests and it took a while for him to be seen.'

She nodded.

I had to respect the confidentiality of each child and even though Amena was living in the same house, it wouldn't be fair on Ralph to share his private medical information with her.

Just then, my mobile rang. It was Shelley.

'How did the protection conference go?' I asked her.

She explained that they'd checked with the school to see if they were aware of Ralph being injured in school time but they didn't recall anything significant happening and there was nothing logged. Also, they couldn't recall a time that Ralph had specified that he was in pain or seemed to be in pain.

'Mrs White said she had noticed that Ralph ran with an odd gait but she had known other children with additional needs to move differently to other kids,' Shelley told me. 'It was one of the things that she wanted to raise with Mum but she never had the opportunity.'

The police were going to ask Renae and Dean to come in for questioning.

'What if they refuse?' I asked.

'It will be made clear to them that if they don't come in voluntarily, they'll be arrested,' Shelley replied.

Knowing what I had seen so far of Dean and Renae, I could imagine their reaction.

'We've also agreed that contact isn't going to happen until we know the results of the police investigation,' said Shelley.

Even parents who were suspected of hurting their children still had a right to see them until they were proven guilty. Sometimes contact did carry on and extra contact workers would be put in the room. But in this case, the police didn't want Renae or Dean having an opportunity to threaten or influence Ralph.

'The one thing I do need to mention, Maggie, is that the police are keen to speak to Ralph,' added Shelley.

My heart sank. I couldn't imagine how he would cope with being brought to a police station and being questioned.

'Do we really want to put him through an interview?' I sighed. 'His speech is so limited, I don't think they would get much out of him.'

'I did explain all of that,' replied Shelley, 'so I think initially they just want to come and talk to him at your house and then take a view.'

'OK,' I said. 'They're welcome to try that.'

I really wished that Ralph could talk and tell them everything that had happened to him but sadly I just couldn't see it happening and I didn't want him to become distressed.

'When do they want to come?' I asked her.

'Well, they did ask if they could come in the next hour or so,' she said. 'They're keen to speak to Ralph before they go round to see Renae and Dean and take them in for questioning.'

'OK,' I agreed.

When I got off the phone, I knew I needed to prepare Ralph although I wasn't going to tell him that it was the police who were coming.

'There's going to be some people coming round to see us in a little while,' I told him. 'What cars could you show them?'

He didn't even react to what I was saying and looked at me blankly.

An hour later, two plain-clothed officers turned up at the door. One was a smiley-looking woman in her thirties and the other was a younger man.

'I'm DC Julie Mitchell and this is my colleague, DC Luke Jones,' the woman told me.

'Come in,' I told them. 'Ralph's just in the living room watching TV. He's still a bit tired after everything that happened at the hospital yesterday.'

'Poor little poppet,' sighed DC Mitchell.

Before they went in to see Ralph, I led them through to the kitchen and made them both a cup of tea.

'I don't know how much you know from his social worker,' I said, 'but Ralph isn't very verbal. He only says a few words and doesn't really speak in long sentences so I don't honestly think you're going to get much from him.'

'We understand that,' nodded DC Jones, 'but we do need to give it a try.'

'I can promise you we'll go really gently with him,' added DC Mitchell. 'And if he shows any signs of distress then we will stop straight away. I've got a five-year-old myself so I know kids can be stubborn,' she smiled.

'Thank you,' I sighed. 'I appreciate that. He's been through such a lot in the past few weeks.'

I led them through to the living room where Ralph was sitting on the floor playing with his cars.

'Ralph, this is Julie and Luke,' I told him. 'They've just popped in to say hello to you. Remember we were talking about which cars you were going to show them?'

Ralph stared up at them with his intense blue eyes.

'Cars,' he repeated, holding out a red Ferrari in his hand.

DC Mitchell smiled.

'Wow, that's a lovely car,' she gasped. 'I bet it goes really fast. Can I have a look at it?'

'Mine,' said Ralph, holding it close to him.

'Just a word of warning, he gets very protective over his cars,' I told her.

DC Jones sat on the sofa while DC Mitchell lowered herself down onto the carpet next to Ralph.

'Actually, Ralph, I've got something in my bag that you might like,' she told him. She fished around in her handbag and pulled out a small plastic helicopter.

'Copter,' nodded Ralph.

'That's right,' she told him, spinning the propellor with her finger. 'You can play with it if you want.'

She held it out to Ralph. At first he hesitated, but then he grabbed it from her.

I wasn't really supposed to be present when the police were talking to or questioning a child. And since Ralph appeared calm and didn't seem to object to either of them being there, I thought I would leave the room.

'I'll leave you to it,' I told them in a quiet voice. 'But I'll be in the kitchen if you need me.'

'Ralph, I'm just going to do some tidying up,' I told him.

I hovered around outside the living-room door just to make sure that he was OK.

DC Mitchell had a kind, gentle manner and Ralph accepted her playing next to him. At first, she chatted away to him about the cars but then she started asking him more specific questions.

'Ralph, do you remember when your leg was really sore?' she asked him gently. 'Do you remember how you hurt it?'

Ralph stared up at her but didn't say anything.

'What about your ribs?' she asked, showing him where her ribs were so he understood. 'Can you remember when it was hurting here?'

Ralph looked down and started moving the Ferrari around the carpet.

'Brrm brrmm,' he said.

DC Mitchell looked at DC Jones and I could see that she was about to take a different tact.

'Ralph, does Daddy play cars with you?' she asked him.

This time Ralph suddenly stopped what he was doing and went very quiet.

'Did Daddy ever hurt you, Ralph?' DC Mitchell asked him.

I peered through the door.

'Did Daddy do something to hurt your leg?'

Ralph paused then he suddenly leapt to his feet. He threw the helicopter and the Ferrari down on the floor and kicked them both, then he picked up the car box and emptied it out all over the carpet.

'Ralph, it's OK,' DC Mitchell soothed.

But he didn't listen. He ran over to the built-in cupboards in the alcove and started picking up photo frames and throwing them onto the floor.

'Ralph, we don't have to talk about Daddy anymore,' DC Mitchell told him.

'No Daddy!' shouted Ralph as he threw a framed photo of me and Louisa on her wedding day onto the fireplace and it smashed on the tiled hearth. 'No Daddy. No!'

Then he swept a vase from the mantelpiece onto the floor.

Worried about more of my things being damaged but also concerned that Ralph would hurt himself, I quickly ran back into the room. As soon as Ralph saw me, he came charging over to me and threw his arms around my waist.

'Sleep at Maggie's, sleep at Maggie's,' he repeated.

'Yes, you're OK, Ralph,' I told him. 'You're going to sleep at Maggie's.'

It was the first time that he'd ever openly showed me any

affection and I could feel his little body shaking in my arms.

'Don't worry, we'll leave it there,' nodded DC Mitchell.

Hopefully now they could see that it was going to be extremely difficult, if not impossible, to get any evidence from Ralph.

I could see the mention of 'Daddy' had really unsettled Ralph. I sat on the sofa with him as he quietly whooped to himself.

'It's OK, we'll see ourselves out,' DC Mitchell told me quietly. 'I hope he's OK.'

'He will be,' I said, stroking his hair.

The next morning I was determined to get Ralph back to school. Despite everything he'd been through over the past couple of days, I knew he needed the routine and the structure more than ever. I think he felt the same as he was surprisingly compliant as I got him dressed into his uniform.

I wanted to have a word with Mrs White but when I dropped Ralph off at school, it was a different teacher waiting outside the classroom. I recognised her as one of the other teachers in Ralph's year.

'Where's Mrs White today?' I asked.

'Oh, she's got a baby scan this morning,' she smiled. 'But she'll be back this afternoon.'

'No problem,' I replied, making a mental note to have a chat to her at pick-up.

I headed home and got on with some cleaning and caught up with some paperwork. Just after lunch, Shelley rang me.

'Any news on Mum and Dad?' I asked.

'Yes,' she said. 'The police couldn't get any answer at the flat last night but they managed to catch them early this morning and they took them in for questioning.

'It went down as we expected,' she continued. 'Lots of swearing and abuse, and Dean tried to punch one of the officers so they had to arrest him.'

She explained that neither of them had been able to provide any reasonable explanation for any of Ralph's injuries.

'Dean said he was clumsy so he must have hurt himself when he was playing in the playground or at school and Renae refused to comment.'

'What happens now?' I asked.

Shelley told me they'd been released without charge for now while the police reviewed the evidence and talked to the Crown Prosecution Service (CPS) about what they could charge them with.

'We know it's unlikely that Ralph's going to be able to give evidence so they just have to decide what they can or can't prove in court,' she sighed.

As I drove to collect Ralph from school a couple of hours later, I went through it all in my mind. Sometimes I looked at him and wished I knew what he was thinking – if only he could express himself a little bit more and tell us exactly what had been going on at home. Maybe in time that would happen?

I was still picking Ralph up five or ten minutes earlier than the other parents. Normally when I arrived, the class was having story time in a circle on the floor. Mrs White finished early and while all the other children were getting their coats and book bags, she'd bring Ralph out to meet me.

But this afternoon, instead of Mrs White, I could see another woman that I didn't recognise. It wasn't the same teacher who I'd dropped Ralph off with that morning.

I waited a few minutes then I knocked on the classroom doors that opened out onto the playground. The woman looked puzzled as she came over to me.

'Can I help you?' she asked. 'Pick-up's not for another five minutes.'

'Is Mrs White still off?' I asked.

'Yes,' she nodded. 'She had a scan this morning but she wasn't feeling too well afterwards so she's not been in today. I'm Mrs Bates, one of the reception teachers, so I've been helping out.'

'I'm sorry to hear that,' I told her. 'I'm actually here to pick up Ralph. I normally come a little bit earlier for him.'

She looked confused.

'Ralph?' she questioned. 'Ralph's not here, I'm afraid. He's already been picked up.'

My chest tightened.

'No, I don't think that's right,' I replied. 'You must be confusing him with another child.'

'No, it was definitely Ralph,' she replied. 'I even checked with the TA when the woman came and she said that Ralph always goes a bit early.'

My blood ran cold.

'Woman,' I gasped. 'What woman?'

'Um, I'm sorry I don't know her name but it was Kirby's mum,' she replied. 'I checked with the TA and she said that she often picked up and dropped off Ralph.'

'Do you mean Bex, Ralph's neighbour?' I asked.

'That's it,' Mrs Bates nodded. 'She said she was his neighbour. They only left about five minutes ago so you might still catch them . . . Is everything all right?' she added, clearly seeing the panic on my face.

'Not really,' I said, rummaging frantically in my bag for my phone. 'I think something terrible has happened.'

THIRTEEN

Searching for Answers

Mrs Bates' voice faded into the background as my head started to spin.

Why on earth had Ralph's old neighbour, Bex, suddenly come to collect him like this, out of the blue?

It just didn't make any sense.

I had so many questions but in my heart, I knew there could only be one reason.

Renae and Dean.

Had they put her up to it? I was convinced they had to be behind this somehow.

My stomach twisted with fear and dread.

'We've got a major problem here,' I said, trying to stay calm. 'I need to see the headteacher ASAP.'

I knew there was no point running out into the street to see if I could see Bex with Ralph and Kirby. I had come in that way through the main gates and I hadn't spotted them. I knew they would probably be long gone by now as they wouldn't want to risk being around when I arrived.

'I'll take you to Miss Loughran's office straight away,' said Mrs Bates, who looked as panicked as I felt. 'I'm so sorry for the mix-up. Ralph happily went with her and the TA said she often did the pick-ups so I didn't realise there was anything amiss. If there was any doubt then I would never have let her take him . . .'

'It's OK, it's not your fault,' I said.

It wasn't really OK but I knew now wasn't the time to go into how this had happened. What we needed to do was to find Ralph – and quickly.

I practically ran round to the school reception where Miss Loughran was already waiting for me outside the office.

'Maggie, I've just heard what's happened,' she told me. 'What can we do?'

'I need to phone Ralph's social worker ASAP,' I told her.

'Of course,' she said. 'Come into my office.'

As I got my mobile phone out of my bag, I realised my hands were shaking.

Please don't be in a meeting, I willed as I dialled Shelley's number.

Thankfully she answered straight away.

'Ralph's been snatched from school,' I told her breathlessly.

'What?' she gasped, shocked. 'What on earth do you mean? Are you sure?'

I explained what had happened.

'Why would his old neighbour pick him up?' she asked.

'All I can think is that Renae and Dean must have put her up to it,' I told her. 'They've got to be behind this.'

'Unfortunately I think you're right,' she replied.

She talked me through exactly what she was going to do.

'I'm going to call the police now and then I can hopefully go with them to the neighbour's flat,' she added. 'Fingers crossed that Ralph is either there or at his own flat next door with his parents.'

'What shall I do?' I asked her.

'Are you OK to wait there at the school, Maggie?' she asked. 'Just in case it's all been a misunderstanding and they turn up.'

'OK,' I said. 'Please keep me posted.'

'I will do,' she replied. 'It's going to be OK, Maggie. We'll find him.'

I admired her positivity and I hoped with every fibre of my being that Shelley was right.

As soon as I got off the phone, Miss Loughran handed me a cup of tea.

'I'm so sorry that this has happened,' she told me. 'I know the teaching staff are all very distressed. As soon as I can, I'll be putting together an incident report to look into what went wrong.'

'It's a genuine mix-up, what with Mrs White not being here,' I sighed. 'The main thing is that we get Ralph back safely as soon as we can.'

'It's really not acceptable,' sighed Miss Loughran. 'School is the one place Ralph should be safe and our safeguarding procedure has been severely lacking.'

I could see how it had happened with Mrs White being off and different staff being in the classroom.

'Hopefully the social worker will find Ralph at Kirby's house,' nodded Miss Loughran.

I nodded but in reality, I wasn't convinced they were going to have any luck. Surely Bex wouldn't pick Ralph up to then take him back to his parents at their flat or keep him at her flat next door? There would be no point as they'd know that's where the police and Social Services would look first.

None of it made any sense.

Over the next forty-five minutes, I drank multiple cups of tea and sat looking at my phone, willing it to ring. But there was still no word from Shelley.

Finally, my mobile rang and I jumped on it.

'Shelley?' I gasped. 'Have you found him?'

'No, I'm afraid we haven't,' she sighed.

My heart sank as she explained what had happened. Police officers had simultaneously knocked on Ralph's old flat and the neighbour's door.

'No one was at Ralph's flat and the police are currently searching it,' she told me. 'Bex was at her flat with her children but there was no sign of Ralph.'

'But did she say why on earth she'd picked him up?'

Shelley explained that Bex had been very tearful.

'Renae came to her and fed her a real sob story,' she told me.

She'd said 'the Social' were taking Ralph away from them and had made up allegations about them and they wouldn't let them see him.

'She completely played on her emotions,' sighed Shelley. 'Bex has been in a similar situation herself in the past so she knows how awful it can be and she said that she just wanted to help Renae out.'

She explained that Renae had persuaded Bex to collect Ralph from school. Then her and Dean had arranged to meet them around the corner.

'They said they were going to take Ralph to a friend's place and just spend some time with him. Then Renae told her they would drop him back to your house.'

'My house?' I questioned. 'But that's nonsense – they don't even know where I live.'

'Well, exactly,' sighed Shelley. 'I don't think they ever had any intention of dropping him back.'

Despite what had happened, I really felt sorry for Bex.

'I don't think Bex realised how much trouble she was going to get herself into by doing this,' added Shelley. 'She was very tearful and shaky and the police have told her in no uncertain terms that she could go to prison for this and face losing her own kids.'

They had explained to her that she could face criminal charges herself for aiding and abetting child abduction.

I was angry at Bex for being so gullible but she hadn't known about Ralph's injuries. I also felt bad as she'd clearly been taken advantage of too.

'Does she have any idea where they might have taken Ralph?' I asked Shelley.

'Unfortunately not,' she sighed. 'All she knows is that they picked Ralph up on the corner in a car. She didn't recognise the person driving and she can't remember the colour or the make or anything about it. She thinks it might have been red.'

My heart sank. Ralph could be anywhere by now and it felt hopeless.

It was like searching for a needle in a haystack.

Shelley explained the police had put an alert out at all of the ports and airports for Ralph, Renae and Dean. They were also knocking on doors in the block of flats to ask if anyone had seen anything.

'What can I do?' I asked Shelley.

'I don't think there's anything more you can do right now,' she replied. 'I think it's best if you go home just in case Ralph somehow does turn up. The police are in touch with Bex and they're doing everything they can to try to trace Ralph.'

'Have they found him?' asked Miss Loughran as I came off the phone. I shook my head.

I explained what had happened.

'Hopefully it's just a matter of time before they track them down,' she said.

She was full of apologies again as I got ready to head home.

'Please keep us posted,' she told me. 'And let me know if there's anything at all the school can do.'

'I will,' I told her. 'You've got mine and Shelley's numbers so please call us if you find anything out or Ralph suddenly turns up.'

'Absolutely,' she nodded.

I drove home in a daze. I felt completely and utterly helpless.

I kept looking at the empty car seat in the back and thinking of poor little Ralph and how confused and scared he must be by everything.

Part of me was terrified that the police and Social Services would never trace them. Surely Renae and Dean wouldn't risk hanging around the local area. They could even be on their way to another country by now . . .

As I pulled up outside my house, I knew I had to work out how to explain what was happening to Amena. I couldn't not say anything as it was obvious that I was upset and Ralph wasn't with me.

She was making a cup of tea in the kitchen when I walked in.

'Hi,' she smiled. 'Do you want a cuppa? Where's Ralph?'

I felt my eyes fill with tears and I took a deep breath.

'Something happened at school today,' I told her.

I explained that Ralph's parents had taken him without permission.

'But where have they taken him?' she asked, her eyes wide.

'We don't know that yet, but his social worker and the police are dealing with it and I'm sure he'll be back very soon,' I told her.

I tried to sound as positive and as hopeful as possible but I could see that she wasn't convinced.

'Poor Ralph,' she sighed. 'I hope he's OK.'

'He will be, flower,' I told her. 'The police will make sure that he's back with us in no time.'

Poor Amena seemed really shaken. The house just felt odd without Ralph. He'd only been with us for just over a month but it felt eerily quiet.

I spent the evening pacing from room to room, unsure of what to do with myself. Shelley had messaged me a couple of times but had said there was no news.

After dinner, while Amena was doing her homework, I took some clean laundry up to Ralph's room. I carefully folded up his little T-shirts and trousers and put them into his chest of drawers.

I stood at his bedroom window and looked out at the street.

'Where are you, Ralph?' I asked out loud.

It was getting dark now and it was raining and I hated to think of him out there somewhere. What was he doing? Was he being taken care of? Was he scared, wondering what was happening to him? Was he hungry and cold?

Worse still, was he being physically hurt? I desperately wanted to know that he was safe.

I lay down on his bed and sobbed. I prayed that Renae and Dean would eventually do the right thing and bring him back.

After having a good cry, I knew I had to pull myself together. Even though Ralph wasn't there, I pulled down the blind in his room and left his bedside lamp on so his room was all ready in case he came back.

Then I went in to say goodnight to Amena.

'Do you think Ralph will be back tomorrow?' she asked, her brow furrowing with worry.

'I hope so,' I nodded.

I couldn't lie to her but, at the same time, I didn't want her to be anxious.

When Amena had gone to bed, I didn't know what to do with myself. I turned on the TV but I couldn't concentrate on anything. I kept checking my phone to see if there were any missed calls even though the volume was on full.

Becky texted me.

Any news?

Nothing sadly, I replied.

Shelley messaged me to say there had been no updates from the police.

Let's catch up first thing in the morning, she told me. *I hope you are OK.*

I was absolutely shattered but I couldn't stop my mind from whirring. I couldn't eat, I couldn't sleep. I didn't know what to do with myself.

And all the time, there was one big fear running through my head.

Would I ever see Ralph again?

FOURTEEN

Safe and Sound

Sitting at the kitchen table, I watched the sun rise as I finished my cup of coffee. It wasn't even 7.30 a.m. yet and I'd already been up a couple of hours. I could hear Amena in the shower and I knew she'd be down shortly for breakfast.

Surprisingly, I'd actually managed to get three or four hours of sleep, which I was immensely grateful for. But the minute I'd woken up, everything that had happened the previous day hit me like a hammer.

Ralph was gone.

Out of habit, I'd wandered into his bedroom and opened his blind. My heart had sunk with sadness as I saw his little bed, untouched and unslept in.

I couldn't stop thinking about him and wondering where and how he was. Was he safe and warm? Was someone somewhere making him breakfast?

It was the not knowing that was driving me crazy.

I took a final swig of coffee and got up to put some bread in the toaster for Amena when she came down. My phone buzzed on the work surface and I quickly lunged for it. I noticed the number on the screen was Ralph's school.

'Hi, Maggie,' said a voice. 'It's Mrs White.'

I knew she must be ringing as she'd obviously heard about what had happened when she'd been off sick yesterday.

'I'm calling about Ralph,' she told me.

'I know,' I sighed. 'It was all a big mix-up. It's not your fault though, you can't help it if you were off. How are you feeling now?' I asked her.

'No,' she said. 'No, it's not that. It's Ralph.'

'What about him?' I asked.

'He's here,' she told me. 'He's at school.'

'What?' I gasped, nearly dropping the phone in shock.

'I've been trying to call the social worker but she's not picking up.'

I listened, stunned, as Mrs White described how she'd arrived at work five minutes ago to find Ralph sitting on the pavement outside the school gates.

'Was there anyone with him?' I asked, worried.

'No, he's on his own,' she told me. 'I'm the first member of staff here so I don't know where he came from or where he's been. I can't get any sense out of him.'

'Is he OK?' I asked.

'I'm not sure,' she replied. 'He's still in his school uniform and he seems a bit agitated. I tried to get him to come into the classroom but he's just running around the playground making that whooping sound that he does.'

'Please could you try and get him to go inside,' I told her. 'But if not, I'll be there as soon as I can. I'll keep trying Shelley too. Just please stay with him,' I told her.

'Of course I will,' she replied. 'I promise you, I won't let him out of my sight. Miss Loughran's on her way in too.'

As I put down the phone, I was still in shock that Ralph had turned up at school like that. I had so many questions but they would have to wait for now. The main thing was, Ralph was there and he was safe. The relief was indescribable.

As I pulled on some jeans and a jumper, I kept dialling Shelley's number but it went straight to voicemail.

I knew she generally didn't start work until 8.30 a.m. so I quickly typed her a message.

Ralph has turned up at school. On my way there now. Plse call me.

Then I rang my fostering agency and told the duty social worker what had happened and that I was on my way to Ralph's school.

Before I left, I went to see Amena.

'I've got some good news,' I told her. 'Ralph has turned up at his school. I'm going to go up there now and collect him.'

'How did he get there?' she asked, amazed.

'I don't know yet,' I replied. 'But at least he's safe.'

'Oh, that's good news,' she smiled.

'It certainly is,' I told her. 'Hopefully he'll be here later when you get back from school.'

I got into the car and before I turned my key in the ignition, I gave Shelley one last try. It went to voicemail again.

On the drive there, I felt really shaky. I didn't think that I would truly believe Ralph was OK and safe until I'd seen him with my own eyes and he'd been properly checked over.

There was so much that we didn't know and I wasn't sure that he would even be able to tell us.

I couldn't get to his school quickly enough. The street outside was still fairly empty so I managed to park straight away, then I ran to the front gates and frantically pressed the buzzer.

'Maggie, it's Miss Loughran,' said a voice over the intercom. 'I'm letting you in now.'

'Thank you,' I said.

I tapped my foot impatiently as I waited while the metal gates slowly creaked open. I squeezed through them and as I ran around the corner, my heart was in my mouth. I desperately scanned the playground, my eyes searching for Ralph.

Sure enough, there was a little figure running round in laps. Mrs White was stood to one side talking to him but he wouldn't keep still.

'Whoop, whoop,' he yelled.

I'd never been so grateful to hear that noise and my whole body sagged with relief.

Ralph looked tired and slightly dishevelled. His uniform was creased and his brown hair was all matted and stuck up at the back.

I didn't want to rush straight over to him and scare him.

Miss Loughran walked across the playground towards me.

'I can't believe he's turned up like this,' she told me. 'What a relief.'

'Neither can I,' I said, unable to take my eyes off him.

Just then my phone rang. It was Shelley.

'I've just picked up your messages,' she said breathlessly. 'How is he?'

I explained that I'd literally just arrived at school.

'I haven't had a chance to talk to him yet but he's here and he seems OK although he's quite agitated,' I told her.

'And no sign of Renae or Dean?'

'None,' I said. 'He turned up on his own. No one knows where he's come from or where he's been yet. He was here waiting at the gates when Mrs White arrived this morning.'

Shelley explained that she was on her way up to the school now as well.

'I've called the police and let them know what's happened so they might arrive before me,' she added.

'OK,' I said.

I was keen to try and get Ralph inside and calm him down before the police arrived. I went over to talk to Mrs White.

'How is he?' I asked her.

'I've tried to talk to him but he won't engage with me,' she shrugged. 'He seems very wound up and jittery.'

I wanted to get Ralph to come to me but he was staring at the ground and not making eye contact.

As he ran, I noticed his bad leg turning in and I shuddered, remembering all of his old injuries.

Please don't let them have hurt him again, I willed.

'Whoop, whoop!' yelled Ralph.

But then as he scampered past, he suddenly looked up and his gaze met mine. He stopped dead in his tracks and I stared into his intense blue eyes. He had dark shadows underneath them and he looked totally and utterly exhausted.

'Hi, Ralph,' I smiled. 'I'm so pleased to see you.'

'Will you . . .' he said in a small voice.

'Will I what, lovey?' I asked him, seeing that he was struggling to get his words out.

'Please help me,' he said in a small voice. 'Sleep at Maggie's house?'

I was taken aback. It was the first proper sentence that Ralph had said to me and I could see the distress and utter despair in his eyes.

'Of course you can sleep at Maggie's house,' I told him. 'Would you like that?'

He nodded.

'Sleep at Maggie's,' he repeated and I felt tears prick my eyes.

Slowly I walked towards him.

'Cars?' he asked me.

'Oh, would you like me to find you some cars?' I said, smiling.

'Cars,' he nodded.

I could see that he was asking for all of the things that made him feel safe.

'I'm sure Mrs White has got some cars in her classroom,' I told him. 'How about we go inside and find some?'

I held out my hand to him and, much to my surprise, he took it.

I gripped his little hand and led him into the classroom.

Mrs White quickly got a big plastic box of vehicles out from one of the cupboards.

'Here you go, Ralph,' she smiled. 'There are lots of cars in there.'

Ralph picked up the box and tipped them all out onto the carpet then he sat down and started sorting through them.

I was so relieved to see he was calming down.

'Would it be OK to get him a drink and a biscuit?' I asked Mrs White.

'Of course,' she nodded. 'I'll nip to the staffroom.'

She came back a few minutes later with a beaker of warm milk and two digestive biscuits.

'Would you like a drink and something to eat, Ralph?' I asked him gently.

He grabbed the beaker straight away and gulped the milk down without pausing for breath. Then he shoved the biscuits into his mouth.

I could tell that he was starving.

'Shall I try and get him some toast or some porridge from the kitchens?' Mrs White asked.

'If you can, that would be great,' I told her.

A few minutes later, Miss Loughran came into the classroom.

'Maggie,' she said quietly to me. 'The police are here.'

I could see DC Julie Mitchell – the officer who had come to question Ralph at my house – standing in the doorway along with another female officer whom I hadn't met before. I left Ralph playing on the carpet and went over to them.

'This is my colleague, DC Helen Jones,' she told me and I nodded. 'I'm so sorry to hear what happened to Ralph. I'm glad he's turned up safely.'

'Me too,' I told her. 'I was going out of my mind with worry.'

'Has he said anything about where he's been or who he's been with?' she asked me.

'Nothing,' I replied. 'He was quite agitated when I got here so I haven't asked him anything yet, to be honest.'

'I understand,' nodded DC Mitchell.

She explained that they'd like to try to speak to Ralph to see if he could give them any clues about where he'd been.

'Our main priority is to find his parents, Renae and Dean,' she told me.

I explained that his teacher had gone to the kitchen to get him some food.

'He's tired and hungry,' I said. 'I know you need to try to find out as much as you can but if you could give him five or ten minutes to have something to eat, I'd really appreciate it.'

'Of course,' DC Mitchell replied.

'Why don't you come with me to my office and I'll get you both a cup of tea?' suggested Miss Loughran.

I knew Ralph just needed a bit of time and space. Mrs White came back with a big plate of toast and jam for him and he tucked straight into it.

'Bless him, he's absolutely starving,' she sighed.

Then he carried on playing with his cars.

Exactly ten minutes later, the police officers came back.

'I'm really not sure how receptive he's going to be,' I warned them.

'Well, we've got to give it a go,' DC Mitchell told me. 'I'm happy for you to stay with Ralph, Maggie, if you'd like to.'

'Yes, please,' I nodded.

I felt like this time I needed to be there after everything Ralph had been through.

Miss Loughran had pulled a couple of extra plastic chairs over to where Ralph was playing on the carpet and the police officers sat down.

'Hi, Ralph,' said DC Mitchell softly. 'My name's Julie. Remember I came to see you at Maggie's house the other day? You showed me your cars.'

Ralph didn't engage with her; in fact, he didn't even look up.

'Ralph, were you with Mummy and Daddy yesterday?' she asked him. 'Did they take you somewhere?'

He carried on playing with his cars.

DC Mitchell looked across at DC Jones as if to suggest that she took over.

'Ralph, my name's Helen,' she told him. 'It's lovely to meet you. Can you tell me about where you were last night?'

Again, Ralph completely ignored her.

It was clear they weren't going to get very far with him. I didn't want to cause Ralph any distress but I knew we needed to get to the bottom of where he'd been so I decided to ask him some questions. He was closest to me and I didn't have anything to lose. I was sure the police wouldn't mind.

'Where did you come from this morning, Ralph?' I asked him casually. 'Which house did you stay at last night?'

He looked up at me.

'Not Maggie's,' he said, shaking his head.

'No, you didn't stay at Maggie's house,' I agreed. 'Where did you stay, Ralph?'

'House,' he told me.

'Oh, you stayed at another house?' I said and he nodded.

'Where was the house that you stayed in?' I asked him.

Ralph shrugged.

'Over there,' he said, pointing out to the playground.

I could see the police officers looking at each other.

'Over there?' I grinned. 'That's the playground. You didn't sleep in the playground, did you?'

He gave me a little wry smile and shook his head.

I tried to make it into a game to extract as much information as I could from Ralph, unsure if it was actually going to lead anywhere.

'Was it a big house that you went to?' I asked him.

He shook his head.

'Was it a nice house?' I asked. 'Did you like it?'

He shook his head firmly.

'Did you have your own bedroom at this house?'

He shook his head again.

'What could you see out of the window of this house, Ralph?' I asked.

He looked at me as if he was thinking for a moment then he pointed to the window. I was puzzled but then I realised what he meant.

'Oh, you could see school?' I asked and he nodded.

The two police officers looked at me as if to acknowledge that I should keep going.

'Ralph, do you think you could show me the house where you were last night?' I asked him gently. 'I'd really like to see it.'

He looked up at me and nodded.

'Come,' he said, holding out his hand to me.

We all stared at each other, unsure of what to do next.

'You go with him and we'll hang back and watch,' DC Mitchell whispered to me under her breath.

I knew young children had no sense of distance or time but the fact that Ralph had got himself to school told me that he must have been somewhere relatively nearby. I was aware this could be a complete wild goose chase but we had to try it.

'Come on then,' I said cheerfully to him. 'You show me this house.'

He seemed quite happy to lead me across the playground and out of the school gates onto the street, then he suddenly stopped as if he was confused. He looked around.

'Was the house this way, Ralph?' I said, gesturing to the right.

He looked at me and shook his head.

'There,' he said, pointing up the left-hand side of the street.

'Did you have a very long walk this morning when you came to school?' I asked.

He shook his head.

Still holding my hand, he led me about two hundred metres up the street that the school was on. On the left-hand side of the road was a parade of shops, which included a newsagent, a laundrette and a pizza takeaway and they all had two- or three-storey flats above them. Then on the other side of the street was a row of 1960's brick houses.

As we walked towards the houses, I could feel Ralph starting to slow down. He suddenly looked scared and he pulled me back by my hand.

'Go back,' he said in a small voice. 'Go back.'

'You want to go back to school?' I asked him and he nodded.

He looked petrified but I knew I needed to ask him one more question, just to be sure.

'Ralph, is the house that you stayed in last night near here?'

He nodded.

Then he pointed across the street to the row of terraces.

'House there,' he said. 'Go back,' he said again, and I could see that he was shaking.

'It's OK, Ralph, we're going to go back to school now, don't worry,' I soothed.

I could see Ralph couldn't get back to the school grounds quickly enough and he practically dragged me down the street.

DC Mitchell and DC Jones had been hanging back behind us.

As we passed them, I quietly muttered: 'He says it's one of those.'

I gestured to the row of around eight houses.

'We'll call for back-up now,' DC Mitchell nodded.

'He might have got it completely wrong,' I warned them.

'Let's see,' she replied.

I didn't know what to think. Ralph's communication wasn't that good; could we rely on a six-year-old's memory? However, it was clear something had frightened him.

The police were handling things now and all I wanted to do was to get Ralph back to the safety of my house as quickly as possible.

FIFTEEN

Daddy's Gone

Shelley had arrived by the time we got back to the school.

'Ralph!' she smiled as we walked into the classroom. 'I'm so pleased to see you!'

I could feel him pressing up against my leg and I knew I needed to get him back to my house as soon as I could; he was exhausted and I didn't want him to still be there when all of the other pupils started arriving for the school day.

'Why don't you play with the cars for two minutes while I chat to Shelley,' I told Ralph gently.

He didn't say anything but he did as I'd asked and sat down wearily on the carpet.

I went over to Miss Loughran and Shelley.

'I think he just showed us some houses that Renae and Dean may have taken him to last night,' I told them. 'They're just up the road.'

'That's great,' replied Shelley.

'The police are there now,' I said.

'Let's hope they find them and they're able to arrest them,' nodded Shelley.

I explained that Ralph seemed hungry and tired and I wanted to take him back to my house.

'Do you think we need to take him to the hospital and get him checked out?' asked Shelley.

I shrugged my shoulders.

'He seems exhausted and agitated but he doesn't seem hurt,' I told her. 'I'll give him a bath and have a good look at him and if I think he's injured in any way or I see any marks on him then I'll get him straight to hospital.'

'Thanks, Maggie,' nodded Shelley. 'I trust your judgement.'

She explained that she was going to stay there as she wanted to talk to the police to find out what was happening.

I was keen to get Ralph home as quickly as I could.

I knelt down on the carpet next to him.

'Ralph, I'm going to take you back to my house now,' I told him.

He nodded and got up straight away.

'I'll keep you posted,' Shelley told me.

I could see Ralph was as keen as I was to leave school. As we walked out of the gates, I glanced up the road and saw a couple of police cars and an ambulance parked outside the row of terraced houses that Ralph had pointed to.

Seeing an ambulance there struck me as odd but thankfully I was parked lower down the street in the opposite direction. I didn't want to risk Ralph seeing his parents or witness a commotion outside the house as they were being arrested.

On the drive home, Ralph was quiet and I could see that he was nodding off. I felt so sorry for him. Whatever had happened last night, he clearly hadn't managed to sleep much.

By the time we pulled up outside my house, his eyes were firmly closed. I felt bad disturbing him so I decided to sit in the car and send a few messages.

I texted Becky and let her know what had happened.

Just got Ralph home. He's been so brave. He showed us what we think is the street where he was last night. Police there now.

There were no updates yet from Shelley or the police but I knew I'd feel a lot safer once Renae and Dean were in custody. I knew they probably weren't aware of where I lived but there was always an element of worry that they'd try to take Ralph again.

I was contemplating carrying Ralph into the house and laying him down on the sofa when his eyes suddenly sprung open.

'Oh,' he said, looking around, blinking. 'Maggie's house.'

'Yes, you're back at Maggie's house, flower,' I told him.

He followed me groggily up the path and we walked straight through to the kitchen.

'Are you still hungry, Ralph?' I asked him. 'Do you want something else to eat?'

'Sausages,' he nodded.

After everything he'd been through, I was desperate to feed him up.

'You're in luck,' I smiled. 'I've got some sausages in the fridge so I'll get them cooking.'

When they were ready, he wolfed them down as well as some toast. Slowly I could see the colour coming back into his cheeks.

'I'm going to run you a lovely warm bath now,' I told him.

I knew I needed to check that there were no marks or obvious injuries on him. I wasn't going to ask him any more questions about last night or his parents as he'd been through enough. I'd only talk about it if he mentioned it himself.

Ralph was so exhausted that he didn't put up any resistance to me getting him undressed. As I took off his school trousers, the smell of stale urine hit me and I could tell that, at some point, he'd wet himself. He'd obviously been left in the same clothes as his skin was red and sore, and my heart ached for him. Thankfully I couldn't see anything else of concern.

After his bath, I put him into some clean clothes and we went downstairs. I got Ralph settled on the sofa with a blanket in case he wanted to have a nap. Sure enough, ten minutes later, he was fast asleep again.

I was determined to let him rest and catch up. I didn't want to dwell on what had happened the night before. He was safe now and that was all that mattered.

I was doing some paperwork when Shelley rang.

'What's happened?' I asked. 'Was it the right street? Did the police find them?'

There was silence on the other end of the phone.

'They found Dean but there was no sign of Renae,' she told me.

But I could hear the hesitation in her voice and I knew instantly that there was something wrong.

'What is it, Shelley?' I said. 'What is it that you're not telling me?'

'I don't know how to say this, Maggie,' she sighed. 'The police did find Dean at the house but I'm afraid he was dead.'

It was a huge shock.

'Dead?' I gasped. 'But how?'

'It looks like a drug overdose,' continued Shelley. 'There'll be a post-mortem but there was drug paraphernalia everywhere and that's what the police believe it looks like.'

I shuddered. I just hoped that Ralph hadn't found him or been there to witness that.

Shelley explained that the house was a council property rented by a man called Martin Smith.

'We don't know who he is or where he is,' she continued. 'We can only assume he's a friend or family member or associate of theirs. The police said the place was filthy and very run-down.'

They had issued a warrant for Renae's arrest in connection with taking Ralph.

Thinking of Ralph, my heart sank.

'What are we going to tell him?' I asked her. 'Do we have to tell him today?'

He'd been through so much in the past twenty-four hours.

'I think so,' Shelley told me. 'There's never going to be a good time to deliver that sort of news and I think he needs to know. We don't know how much he saw when he was at the house.'

I felt sick. He was only six; you couldn't really get into the ins and outs of Dean's death with a child of that age.

'I know it's your job to tell him but please can I be there with him when you do it?' I asked.

'Of course you can,' replied Shelley.

I explained he was asleep at the moment.

'I'd rather do it sooner rather than later, so if it's all right with you, I'll head over to you now?' she asked.

'Whatever you think is best,' I responded.

After I'd hung up, I went to check on Ralph, who was still fast asleep on the sofa. I felt like crying; he'd faced so many challenges in the past few weeks and I knew he had a complicated relationship with Dean, his stepfather. Whenever anyone had talked about him or asked about him, Ralph had only ever displayed what I believed was fear and anger. I was worried about what kind of effect the news was going to have on him.

I sat down next to him on the sofa and stroked his hair. His eyes gently fluttered open.

'Hello, sleepyhead,' I smiled. 'Shelley's coming over to talk to you now.'

He just rolled over and stared into the distance.

Half an hour later, Shelley arrived. Firstly we went into the kitchen and I made us both a cup of tea.

'I think we need to be very logical and explain it to him in a really straightforward way,' Shelley told me.

'I agree,' I nodded.

Because of his suspected learning difficulties, I was never sure how much Ralph actually understood anyway.

He was sitting on the sofa watching cartoons when Shelley and I went in and sat either side of him.

I turned off the TV. Shelley cleared her throat and began to speak.

'Ralph, you've been such a brave boy,' she told him. 'You showed us where the house was that Mummy and Daddy took you to last night and you were right. Mummy wasn't there but we did find Daddy.'

She paused.

'Unfortunately, when we found Daddy, he was dead.'

Ralph stared straight ahead.

'Do you understand what I'm telling you, Ralph?' she asked him. 'I'm afraid that Daddy has died. That means he's not alive anymore.'

Ralph turned and looked at Shelley and before I could stop him, he lunged at her. Shelley let out a yelp as Ralph grabbed her long blonde hair with both of his hands and started yanking it.

'Ralph!' I shouted. 'Please stop that now! We don't pull someone's hair!'

'Whoop! Whoop! Whoop!' he yelled, violently pulling it again and again.

I quickly got behind him and used a technique that I'd been taught on a training course. If a child was pulling hair, you pressed their hands against the person's scalp to stop it from hurting. However, as I did that, Ralph spun round and lunged at me instead.

Pain seared through my scalp as he yanked on my hair. I used the same technique and pressed my hands on his then eventually I managed to peel him off me.

I grabbed the blanket that Ralph had been covered with while he was sleeping and wrapped him in it. Then I put my arms around him.

'It's OK, Ralph,' I soothed as I held him close. 'I know the news about Daddy is very sad.'

I could feel him trembling in my arms.

Shelley looked shaken.

'Are you OK?' I asked her quietly and she nodded.

'Why don't you go into the kitchen and wait for me there

and I'll sit with Ralph for a few minutes,' I told her.

She nodded again and looked relieved to be leaving the room.

'It's all right,' I soothed. 'You're OK. Maggie's here.'

Eventually I felt his body go limp in my arms. We sat in silence for the next ten minutes until I could tell that he was truly relaxed.

'Are you OK, Ralph?' I asked him and he nodded.

'I'm going to put the TV back on for you and I'm going go and have a chat to Shelley,' I told him.

I went into the kitchen where Shelley was sitting with a cup of tea.

'I'm so sorry about that,' I told her. 'I think that was Ralph's way of expressing his shock and upset.'

'It was a bit of shock for me too when he went for me,' she sighed.

'He seems to have calmed down now thankfully,' I replied.

His little head must be all over the place as he struggled to process what had happened.

'What happens now?' I asked.

Shelley explained that the police would continue to investigate Dean's death and keep looking for Renae.

'From a Social Service's point of view, we've got a LAC review next week.'

A LAC (Looked After Child) review was a meeting where all the people involved in a child's care got together to discuss the next steps. Ralph's case had suddenly taken a very swift turn and we all needed to talk about where we were going to go from here.

'When do you think I should take him back to school?' I asked Shelley.

'Whenever you think he's ready,' she replied.

My fear was that he would suddenly associate school with being in that house and feeling unsafe.

'It all feels like such a mess,' I sighed. 'How much more can one little boy cope with?'

Suddenly there was an almighty crash. Shelley and I looked at each other in panic.

I got up and sprinted into the living room.

The first thing that hit me was the smell.

'Oh no,' gagged Shelley. 'That's disgusting.'

Ralph had pooed in the middle of the carpet and was busy smearing it all over the furniture and the walls. I noticed the TV screen was smashed and I realised that he'd thrown his glass of water at it.

'Whoop! Whoop! Whoop!' he chanted and my heart sank.

SIXTEEN

Fight or Flight

There was only one way to describe the week that followed and that was living hell. After everything Ralph had gone through after being taken from school by his parents and then being told that Dean had died, Ralph's behaviour had deteriorated to the point that it was the worst that it had ever been.

None of us knew what he had been through that night after being snatched from school or how much he understood, but he was clearly in stress mode – or what professionals called fight or flight. It meant that his little body was in a state of constant fear that triggered the release of stress hormones like adrenaline and cortisol. This response gets the body ready to either run from or fight the danger. It must have been exhausting for Ralph to constantly be in that state and it also left him more reactive to day-to-day situations, which explained his decline in behaviour.

There were temper tantrums and constant oppositional behaviour. Anything that I asked him to do, Ralph would say no to and his destruction had reached a new level. I would put a plate, a bowl or a cup in front of him and he'd pick it up and hurl it at the wall. Even though I replaced everything breakable with plastic, there was often food everywhere, and milk and juice dripping down the walls. I felt as if I was constantly cleaning. I was also very aware of how Amena was feeling living in this constant state of upheaval. However, I explained to her how unsettled Ralph was feeling right now and that his behaviour was a reaction to his emotions and thankfully, although she didn't necessarily like it, she understood. Once again, I was amazed by her maturity.

Unless I was walking along with Ralph and holding his hand at all times, he would grab anything that he could and throw it, tear it or smash it. My house looked rather bare as I'd had to put anything breakable or precious high up or out of sight so he couldn't get to it.

I bought him some simple picture books about death as I thought it might help his understanding of what had happened to Dean if we put it in a visual way for him. One night he was in bed and I was reading *My Daddy Died* to him. I went to get him a cup of milk, and when I came back, he'd ripped out all the pages and thrown them on the floor.

His soiling had reached new levels too. I'd spend hours cuddling him in a blanket as it was the only thing that seemed to calm him and make him feel safe, but he'd wee and poo on me. He had reverted to going to the toilet on the floor too. It was as if the previous weeks with me had never happened and I was dealing with that scared, traumatised little boy who had walked through my door in September.

It was distressing and, above all, absolutely exhausting.

I knew that all I could do was try to keep everything

calm and consistent. However, after everything that he'd been through, I knew it was going to take time.

Louisa and Edie came round one afternoon to see us after Louisa had finished work.

'I haven't seen you for ages and I wondered how you were?' she asked.

'OK,' I told her. 'Things have been a little bit challenging in the past few weeks.'

'I'm not surprised after everything poor Ralph went through,' she sighed. 'Have the police or Social Services found his mum yet?'

'Not that I know of,' I replied.

Edie was showing Ralph the doll she was playing with and I was watching him like a hawk.

'Ralph, make sure you have a drink,' I told him, trying to distract him away from her.

He came over to get his plastic beaker of water. In the meantime, Edie had gone over to the toy garage that Ralph had been playing with.

Before I could stop him, Ralph marched over to her.

'No!' he shouted. 'Mine!'

Then he poured his full beaker of water over Edie's head.

Louisa gasped and it was as if time stood still for a moment.

Edie blinked in shock, as the water soaked her hair and ran down her face. I could see her bottom lip quivering.

Louisa quickly stepped in.

'Oh, you've had a shower in the kitchen, Edie. That's silly, isn't it? You don't have a wash in the kitchen! Let's go up to the bathroom and dry you off with a towel.'

It diffused the situation enough that Edie didn't cry, but she looked a bit bemused as Louisa quickly led her upstairs.

'Thank you,' I mouthed.

I turned to Ralph.

'We don't tip water over people,' I told him. 'That isn't very kind. Help me clean it up please.'

Ralph didn't say anything but I mopped up a bit of the water then I handed him the cloth.

'No!' he said defiantly, throwing it onto the floor.

I didn't have time to say anything else as a couple of minutes later, Louisa and Edie came back down.

Edie was very clingy and wouldn't let go of Louisa. When Ralph came anywhere near her, she buried her head in Louisa's top and seemed genuinely scared of him.

Her reaction seemed to fuel Ralph's anger and he started kicking the dolls' house Edie had been playing with earlier and throwing the dolls around.

'No, no, no!' yelled Edie, getting upset again. 'Naughty!'

'I think it's best if we go,' Louisa said to me.

'I'm so sorry,' I sighed. 'Ralph's going through a lot at the moment.'

'Don't worry,' she told me. 'It's going to take time.'

That night Louisa called.

'I'm sorry again about today,' I told her.

'It's not your fault,' she told me.

She explained that Edie had told Charlie about what had happened with the water.

'I told him about Ralph's behaviour lately and he said he doesn't think Edie should be around him,' she said.

'What do you mean?' I asked, though I guessed what was coming.

'Well, I mentioned to Charlie how he's lashed out a few times and I think he's just worried Edie will get hurt if she's in the firing line,' she explained.

'Oh gosh, that's the last thing I would want to happen,' I told her.

'I told Charlie that but he doesn't want to take the risk,' she replied.

I was mortified but I completely understood.

'I suppose that means I'm not going to see a lot of you if Ralph can't be around,' I sighed.

'Well, I've got my day off so when Ralph's at school you can have Nana and Edie time then,' Louisa said reassuringly.

'I know, lovey,' I replied. 'It just feels so all-consuming these days.'

All I could hope was that his behaviour would start to calm down. The LAC review was being held in a few days so hopefully we would have more of a plan for Ralph then.

But the destructive behaviour continued.

Ralph's bedroom was now very bare and sparse as he'd destroyed pretty much anything he could get his hands on. There were holes in the walls where he had gouged out the paint and plaster with his fingers; he'd tried to pull the light down by standing on the bunk bed and he'd smashed the lamp. He'd also been throwing himself off the top bunk so I'd had to dismantle the bunk beds for his own safety.

The carpet in his room had become so sodden with urine, it was past the point of me being able to clean it properly, so I'd had to rip it up and replace it with carpet tiles. Now when Ralph weed or pooed on the floor, I'd replace each tile when they got too damaged. It was cheap, heavy-duty industrial-style material but I knew it was necessary in order to maintain a decent level of hygiene.

At night, there were so many times that Ralph went into the bathroom and trashed all our toiletries, and I knew Amena was terrified that he was going to get into her room again and destroy it. I soon realised there was only one solution – to get a handyman to come round and put a bolt on the outside of every door. They were high enough up so that Ralph couldn't reach them but Amena and I could. It meant Ralph couldn't get into any of the rooms without me being with him, and Amena could go to school without worrying that Ralph might go into her room and destroy her things. For safeguarding reasons, I never put locks on the inside of rooms as I needed to know I could have access to them at all times.

'It's like being in a prison,' Amena sighed, unbolting the living-room door so she could watch TV.

'I'm sorry, flower,' I said. 'It's just what we need to do at the moment to keep Ralph safe and also to protect our things.'

I knew all I could do was to carry on Ralph's routine and make him feel as safe and secure as I could and hope, that in time, his behaviour would settle down again. He'd been assessed by an educational psychologist at school and had also been seen by a paediatrician for an autism assessment, but we were still waiting for those reports. However, his behaviour had deteriorated significantly since then.

It all felt relentless. Ralph had started waking up at 3 or 4 a.m. and refusing to go back to sleep. One morning it was 2.30 a.m. when he started banging and crashing about.

I didn't want him to disturb Amena so I took him downstairs and we sat on the sofa.

'On,' said Ralph pointing at the TV but I shook my head.

'We're not having the TV on, it's sleep time,' I told him.

I didn't want him to start thinking he could get up whenever he wanted and I would make it fun for him. By putting the television on, I'd be signalling to him that this behaviour was acceptable. We both needed him to sleep so all I could do was wait it out.

I went to get him a drink of milk. When I came back into the living room, my heart sank. The carpet next to the sofa was sodden and I could tell by the smell that he'd weed on it.

I soaked it up with some kitchen roll but I just didn't have the energy to clean it properly right then.

'We're going to sit here and wait until you're ready to go to sleep,' I told him.

Many times, I felt my head nodding but I knew I needed to force myself to stay awake and supervise Ralph.

Finally I could see his eyes starting to close.

'It's time to go back to bed now,' I said.

I led him back up to his room.

'Ralph, it's night-time,' I told him firmly. 'You need to go to sleep.'

However, it was 4 a.m. before I finally heard him stop making any noise. My alarm went off two and a half hours later. I walked into Ralph's room to find him wide awake, with poo smeared all over the walls.

I felt like crying.

'Right, I need to put you in the shower,' I told him.

Everything felt like a constant battle and I was exhausted. I knew Ralph must have been too but I was determined to get him to school as he needed the security and predictability of the routine.

Even getting him dressed took forever now.

'Can you put your socks on now, please?' I asked him when he was clean.

It was something that he'd been perfectly able and willing to do before and didn't need any help with. Now, like everything else, he refused.

'No!' he said, pushing the socks away.

I tried a different approach.

'Are your toes cold? Socks would make your feet nice and warm.'

'No!' he repeated.

I brought his socks over to him.

'Ralph, if we're going to take you to school then you need to put your socks on,' I said firmly.

I leant over and tried to slip one of his socks over his bare foot.

'No!' yelled Ralph, flinging his hand back and hitting me in the eye.

I yelped as pain seared through my eyeball. I knew he hadn't done it deliberately but my eye was watering and I knew it was going to be bruised.

I took a deep breath. I was going to get him to school whatever it took, even if that meant going to school with no shoes or socks on.

After breakfast, it was time to get him into the car, which had also turned into a nightmare. I couldn't ask Louisa to come every morning but I had to make sure it was safe for both of us. I put him in the car seat with the five-point harness, which I always made sure was as tight and secure as possible.

Ralph liked holding cars in his hands but I couldn't risk him throwing them at me when I was driving. So one evening, I'd spent hours cutting car shapes out of felt and stitching them together and stuffing them to make soft toy cars. If he was going to throw them, it wouldn't matter as they were soft and spongy.

'These cars are really special ones,' I'd told him. 'So you're only allowed them when you're in the car.'

Thankfully it had seemed to work.

'Shall we go to Maggie's car and see Ralph's special cars?' I asked him.

He wriggled around as I tried to buckle him into his car seat but when he saw the cars, he grabbed them and instantly calmed down.

I looked in the rear-view mirror at my eye, which was still smarting. It was bloodshot and I could see I was going to end up with a huge bruise.

When I pulled up at school, I took a deep breath and summoned all of my energy for the next stage, which was getting Ralph to the classroom door. This had been a struggle lately too.

His behaviour had also deteriorated significantly at school. Before Ralph came into my care, the teachers had been forced to deal with him because they knew if they rang Renae, they'd get no response. But pretty much every day I was being called to go and pick him up. I could see Mrs White was at the end of her tether too.

'Morning,' I said to her as I led Ralph up to the classroom door.

'Another bad night?' she asked as I said goodbye to him.

'I'm afraid so,' I nodded. 'He's probably going to be very tired as he hasn't slept much.'

'OK,' she nodded. 'I'm sorry about that but thanks for letting me know.'

As I walked back to the car, I was wracked with guilt that I felt so relieved. It was so full-on when Ralph was at home that I couldn't leave him alone for a moment, so I clung onto the brief time that I had on my own during the day.

By the time I drove back, I felt exhausted. I would have loved nothing more than to have a lie down but there was so much to clean up – there was wee on the living-room carpet and Ralph's bedroom was a mess too.

Wearily, I filled a bucket with hot water and grabbed the antiseptic spray. I was just about to carry it upstairs and start the clean-up when my phone rang.

My heart sank when I realised it was Miss Loughran.

'I'm sorry, Maggie,' she said apologetically. 'I'm afraid you need to come and get Ralph.'

She explained that his behaviour had become increasingly unmanageable.

'Mrs White simply can't keep him safe as well as try to teach twenty-nine other children. It's just not possible.'

He had been at school less than an hour. I'd reached the end of my tether and I felt like crying.

'Please can you just give me an hour and then I can come and collect him?' I begged her. 'I've got so much to clean up here and I can't do it once Ralph's around.'

'I know it's difficult, Maggie, but we really can't manage him when he's like this,' she told me. 'I have to think of my staff and the other pupils' safety. Ralph's on his own with a

TA in an empty classroom at the moment but he's not calming down,' she added.

'OK,' I sighed. 'I'll be there as soon as I can.'

I put the phone down and burst into tears.

I sat down at the kitchen table and rang Becky.

Through my tears, I told her what had happened.

'My eye is killing me, my house is a mess, I've hardly slept and Ralph has soiled everywhere. If I go and get him now, there's no chance of me being able to clear it up. I can't even have my granddaughter round because her parents think it's unsafe for her to be near Ralph and I can't help but agree with them.'

I let out a gut-wrenching sob.

'I can't do this anymore,' I snivelled.

Becky explained that the agency had a support worker available who could come round.

'I know she doesn't know Ralph, but she could go and pick him up from school and take him to a park for a couple of hours so at least you have more time to clean up?' she suggested.

Both agencies and Social Services had support workers who could step in and give carers a bit of a break, or sometimes they would do some specific work with children such as talking therapy or with older children, preparing them to leave the care system and live independently.

I just wasn't sure it was the right thing for Ralph at this time.

'I'm not sure how that would go,' I replied. 'It might stress him out or upset him even more to have a stranger collect him.'

Talking to Becky, and just knowing there was help available if I needed it, calmed me down. Having a support worker to come round and sit with Ralph and play cars with him would give me time to clean up or do things in the house.

'I think I'll be OK today,' I sniffed. 'But in the future, it's good for me to know that option is there.'

'As long as you're sure, Maggie?' asked Becky. 'I've never heard you so upset.'

'I'll be OK,' I sighed. 'I'm just finding it really hard and the lack of sleep doesn't help.'

'Things will get better,' she told me.

'I know,' was all I could reply.

More than anything in the world, I really wanted to believe her.

SEVENTEEN

Secrets of the Past

Looking around the table, there were quite a few of us squeezed into the office at Social Services for Ralph's Looked After Child (LAC) review. They were all familiar faces – Miss Loughran was there, Shelley, DC Julie Mitchell, as well as my supervising social worker, Becky, and Shelley's boss, Danielle. Ralph was at school but I was constantly checking my phone in case I was suddenly called to collect him.

Leading the meeting was a man called Mark, who had recently been appointed Ralph's Independent Reviewing Officer, otherwise known as an IRO. An IRO was a person who worked for Social Services; normally it was a trained social worker who wasn't directly involved in the case. It was the IRO's job to represent the child and make sure every decision made was in their best interests.

Mark was a very intellectual-looking man in his fifties with round wire glasses and cords.

'It's clear from reading through the files that Ralph has been through an awful lot,' he began. 'I'm not even sure where to start.'

'I can give everyone a summary if you like?' suggested Shelley.

She went over what had happened – how Ralph had come into the care system and gone through two foster carers before he'd ended up at my house. She talked about the issues we'd had with his birth parents at contact, the long list of historic injuries that the doctors had found and then how Ralph had been snatched by his parents from school.

'So is Dean Ralph's biological father?' asked Mark.

'He's actually his stepdad but he's the only father that Ralph's ever known and he knows him as "Daddy",' explained Shelley. 'Renae refused to give us any information about Ralph's biological father; he's never been in his life and in fact she said she wasn't sure who he even was.'

'And I believe that sadly Dean has recently been found dead?' asked Mark.

'That's correct,' nodded DC Mitchell.

She explained that the toxicology report had come back as well as the post-mortem results and it was clear that Dean had died of an overdose, with multiple drugs and high levels of alcohol found in his system.

'And what about Renae?' Mark asked.

'She's gone AWOL and no one has managed to trace her as yet,' sighed Shelley. 'The police have a warrant out for her arrest. The benefits office is aware but there has been no sign of her and she hasn't been back to the flat as far as we know.'

'Do the police think that she's come to any harm?' queried Mark.

'There's no indication of that and we're hopeful that she will turn up eventually,' replied DC Mitchell.

She also pointed out that Dean's body was still in the mortuary.

'Without Renae, we're still trying to trace his next of kin and we're having difficulty locating family members,' she added.

'This has been a common problem all along,' nodded Shelley.

Shelley explained that, after weeks of digging, they were only just piecing together information about the family.

'What has become clear, the more we have found out, is that the three of them moved around the country a lot, which probably explains why Ralph has never been on any Social Service's radar.

'There were no medical records for Ralph, he was never registered with a GP. The only school he seems to have attended is the one that he's currently at.

'When Renae married Dean six years ago, she took his surname. Most of their benefits were in Dean's name.'

'Oh, I didn't realise that they were married,' I told her.

'Neither did we,' Shelley replied.

She went on to explain that it was only after weeks of emails, phone calls and being passed around many different local authorities, that they had managed to discover Renae's maiden name and searched under that.

'What that brought up is a whole other can of worms,' Shelley told us. 'And this is information that I have only just found out this morning before coming to this meeting . . .'

What she said next was a huge shock that I certainly hadn't been expecting.

'Nine years ago, Renae had two children removed from her care by Social Services due to drug and alcohol abuse,' said Shelley.

She explained that it was a local authority at the other end of the country and the children were two girls – one had been a young baby at the time and the other girl was two years old.

'When she was pregnant with Ralph, Renae and Dean got married and she took his surname,' Shelley continued. 'That, combined with the fact that they constantly moved around during her pregnancy, and that Renae wasn't registered with a particular hospital and didn't see a midwife, meant she managed to avoid being on Social Service's radar as she should have been.'

I was stunned at the news that Ralph had two half-sisters that he knew nothing about.

'Where are the girls now?' I asked.

'They were both adopted by the same couple,' Shelley said. 'I only got their details this morning so I haven't made contact with them yet.'

The girls were eleven and nine now.

Shelley explained that the adoption department of the family's local Social Services would give the adoptive parents the information that their daughters had been found to have a half-sibling. They didn't have to act on that information or do anything about it, but it was part of their adoptive daughters' life story and so Social Services had an obligation to pass it on.

'It might be that they want the girls to meet Ralph or it may be something they want to wait and tell the girls in the future when they're older, but let's wait and see,' said Shelley.

We also needed to talk about what the short-term plan was for Ralph.

'Well, because we can't currently locate Renae and, given everything that's happened in the past few weeks, she's unlikely to be given custody of Ralph, we feel that the only way forward is a full care order,' said Shelley.

Going forward, that meant Social Services would have parental responsibility for Ralph.

'Maggie, are you OK to continue fostering Ralph while we decide on a long-term plan?' Shelley asked.

'Yes, that's fine,' I nodded. 'I have mentioned to Becky that I might require some ongoing support from my agency as some days it feels quite overwhelming, but I'm hopeful that Ralph's behaviour will start to settle down again.'

My head was still reeling from the news about Ralph's half-siblings when Mark turned to Miss Loughran to get her thoughts on Ralph.

'I'm afraid we're sadly reaching the point where the school just can't manage Ralph and his behaviour,' she said. 'I know he was assessed by an educational psychologist recently and we're still waiting for that report. However, I do feel the only solution is to start looking for an alternative provision.'

Mark turned to me.

'What do you think, Maggie?' he asked.

'I agree,' I nodded. 'We're at a point where Ralph is only going to school for a couple of hours a day at the very most because they just can't cope with him.'

I explained that his behaviour had deteriorated since he was snatched from school.

'He had been making really good progress,' I added. 'He was much calmer and he was using the toilet and able to concentrate. However, since what happened with his parents, we seem to be back to square one again.'

I said how I hoped that with stability, routine and consistency, Ralph would start to settle down.

'But even so, I do feel that in the long term, a specialist provision would be better for him,' I added. 'It's clear Ralph has some sort of learning or developmental difficulties. His speech isn't what it should be for a six-year-old and, as yet, he's unable to read and write.'

Miss Loughran nodded.

We also talked about how Ralph had had an autism assessment with a paediatrician and was waiting to start speech and language therapy.

'While we're waiting for the outcome of the assessment, it seems like everyone is in agreement that we need to start looking for some alternative provision,' nodded Mark, taking notes.

LAC reviews were always long and sometimes hard-going but it was always worth it in the end. It was always useful for all of the different agencies involved in a child's care to be able to share information with each other. I was also someone who liked a plan so it was helpful for me to know at least what the next few weeks had in store.

A few days later, Shelley called.

'Have you had any more news about Ralph's half-sisters?' I asked her.

'No, it's not that,' she replied. 'It's Renae.'

She explained that Renae had turned up drunk at the benefits office in town. They had called the police and she had been arrested.

'She's currently being questioned and they said they'd give me a call when they know more.'

Despite everything that had happened, it was a relief to know that she was OK as I'd had an underlying worry that she'd had an overdose like Dean and the police just hadn't found her yet.

Later that night, Shelley rang back. DC Mitchell had just called her to let her know what had happened.

'It took so long because they had to wait for her to sober up,' she told me.

'Did she say much?' I asked.

'Oh yes, lots,' replied Shelley. 'Now Dean is dead, she was apparently very chatty.'

Shelley explained how she had blamed him for everything.

'During her interview, she admitted that Dean had used Ralph as a punch bag. She said that he regularly hit him, kicked him, locked him in his room for hours, even flushed his head down the toilet. It sounds horrific, Maggie.'

My heart broke for Ralph and everything he'd been through. I thought back to when Ralph had first arrived at my house and how scared he'd been when I'd tried to get him to flush the toilet and how he'd hated the feeling of the water on his face in the shower. It all made sense now.

Part of me felt angry too that Dean would never be punished for the violence he'd inflicted on a vulnerable little boy.

'According to Renae, it was all Dean,' sighed Shelley. 'Obviously it's easy for her to say that now that he's not here.'

'But, even so, she was aware of what Dean was doing to her son,' I sighed. 'Why didn't she get help or tell someone?'

'Well, exactly,' sighed Shelley. 'Renae said she was scared to go to the police because she knew Social Services would get involved and they'd take Ralph away from her when they found out her other kids had been taken into care.'

Regardless of the circumstances, I didn't know how any parent could sit back and let their child be treated like that. However, the fact was we were only ever going to get Renae's version of events. And it was potentially much easier to put all the blame on Dean now he wasn't there to defend himself.

Shelley explained that they'd charged her with neglect and child abduction.

'The CPS feel that they can't prove that Renae hurt Ralph or was involved in hurting Ralph but she knew that Dean had and she didn't seek medical attention for her son,' added Shelley.

My heart ached for Ralph and the fear he must have felt in what should have been his safe place. The hardest thing for me was knowing that he didn't have the ability to tell anyone what was going on – he just didn't have the words and was too scared to speak out anyway.

How could anyone be so cruel to a child? It was just unbearable.

EIGHTEEN

Family Ties

A few days after the LAC review, Shelley called me.

'I've finally had the reports from the paediatrician and the educational psychologist through,' she told me.

She explained that Ralph had been diagnosed with autism spectrum disorder or ASD.

'I think it was what we all expected,' she added. 'How do you feel about it, Maggie?'

'It's a relief,' I agreed. 'It was always clear to me that Ralph needed some extra support.'

A proper diagnosis would open up lots of different options for Ralph and enable us all to have a better understanding of his behaviour.

'The educational psychologist echoes what was decided at the LAC review,' she told me. 'She's also recommended that Ralph's needs would be better served in an alternative provision rather than at mainstream school. That way he can get the extra support and the one-to-one attention that he needs.'

The school were currently looking into several different options for him. Miss Loughran had been telling me about Clover Woods, a school based in woodland where most of the learning took place outdoors.

'I'm really hoping the school in the woods has space for him,' I told her. 'I think Ralph would love it.'

The paediatrician had also suggested another appointment to discuss medication.

'Autism isn't an illness, but there can be treatments to support the development of new skills and behaviours,' said Shelley. 'Medication can often be helpful if he's suffering from anxiety or struggling to sleep.'

'I think let's see how we go first,' I told her. 'I don't want to jinx it but things are getting better.'

I wasn't averse to medication if it could help improve things for Ralph but I had also seen a slow calming down of Ralph's behaviour. Since the LAC review he had only been doing two hours at school every morning and I think knowing that he didn't have to do a full day had helped to ease his stress.

I'd focused all of my time and energy into making Ralph feel as safe and secure as I could. I'd kept everything at home peaceful and quiet and had tried not to let anything unexpected happen. So even if it was something as simple as Shelley coming round in the afternoon, I'd talk about it in the morning and keep mentioning it to him rather than leaving it and her just turning up without warning.

I'd also created some picture charts as I thought Ralph might have a better understanding of things if they were presented to him visually rather than verbally. I'd used them with autistic children before.

I printed out some pictures and stuck them in clear plastic pockets with Velcro on the back. Then I'd stick them on a picture board to show Ralph what he was doing that day.

In the mornings, I'd go through the cards, showing him pictures of what was going to happen.

'You're going to have breakfast, then you'll wash your face and brush your teeth and then you'll get dressed,' I'd explain.

Then when he completed each task, I would take that card off the picture board and praise him.

I did the same at bedtime so he'd know exactly what was going to happen – that it was a bath, followed by teeth, followed by pyjamas and a story – and I'd always try to stick to the same routine.

Some days he'd completely ignore it or rip the pictures up and throw them on the floor but I persevered and most of the time it seemed to work well.

I also came up with lots of sensory activities that we could do at home together, which I knew were good for children who were anxious or in fight or flight mode.

One afternoon, I decided to try painting wooden lolly sticks. I put lots of newspaper down on the work surface and five pots of different-coloured paints and sat Ralph on a stool at the breakfast bar.

'We're going to paint these lolly sticks a pretty colour,' I told him.

'No!' he shouted, raising his hand and swiping all the paint off the work surface and onto the floor.

'Never mind,' I said, my heart sinking at yet another mess to clean up. 'Come and help me to clean it up, Ralph.'

I wasn't perfect. I didn't have endless patience and sometimes I did have to stop myself from yelling at him. However, I also knew that although yelling might make me feel better in the moment, ultimately it could cause damage to the relationship I'd built with Ralph, who'd had a lifetime of people screaming and yelling at him. That was always enough to make me appear calm, even though I wasn't on the inside.

I was determined not to give up on the lolly sticks, so we tried it again another day. This time I'd learnt my lesson and I'd got some thick poster paint that couldn't be spilt.

'We're going to paint some lolly sticks,' I told him. 'What colour would you like to paint them?'

This time I was going to leave the decision-making to Ralph and he could choose just one colour.

'That,' he said, pointing to the blue pot.

'Good choice,' I said. 'I like blue.'

I painted one stick to show him how it was done.

'Ralph's turn,' I smiled.

Much to my amazement, for the next ten minutes, Ralph painted at least twenty lolly sticks. I could see the concentration on his little face as he dabbed them with his paintbrush. I stood next to him while he worked and gently stroked his arm to give him reassurance that I was there.

'Well done,' I told him. 'When they're dry, we're going to go and stick them on the fence in the garden and make some patterns.'

I'd learnt that Ralph seemed to like it when I gave him control. Later that afternoon, we went outside.

'Ralph, put some glue on the sticks,' I told him but he shook his head.

'Maggie do it,' he said.

So I smeared glue on the sticks and Ralph directed me where to stick them.

'There,' he said, pointing to the fence panels. 'And there.'

Making things was also a good way of boosting children's self-esteem. Now whenever we looked out the kitchen window, we'd see Ralph's lolly sticks on the fence and I'd point them out to him.

'Remember when you painted those, Ralph?' I'd say to him. 'You helped me do the gluing and you made such pretty patterns on the fence.'

'Stick,' he nodded. 'Blue. Glue.'

'That's right,' I'd smile. 'You did so well. I think they look really lovely.'

Play-Doh was a good sensory activity too. It was tactile and squishy and it didn't matter if Ralph threw it or ripped it. He seemed to enjoy the feel of it in his hands as he pulled it apart and rolled it into balls.

One day I read some research in a newsletter from my fostering agency that said rhythm and vibrations really helped to soothe and calm children. I'd never thought of it before but I knew I had a couple of toy drums in the loft so I got them out and figured we could give them a go.

Ralph eyed me suspiciously as I sat on the floor and bashed out a simple pattern on my drum.

'Now Ralph do it,' I told him.

'No!' he shouted, kicking his drum away so it rolled across the rug.

I tried again.

'Maggie's turn,' I said, bashing out another simple rhythm.

'Ralph's turn now,' I repeated.

Ralph was lying on the floor, looking totally disinterested.

'No!' he shouted.

I refused to give up and kept on tapping my drum and encouraging Ralph to have a go on his. Finally, if a little reluctantly, I got him to tap his little hands on the drum.

'Wow,' I smiled. 'Listen to that. Can you do it again?'

Ralph bashed his hands down on the drum to make a loud boom and he gave a little smile of satisfaction.

'That's it,' I nodded. 'Can you copy Maggie?'

Soon he was trying to copy the pattern that I'd come up with and I could see that he was engrossed. It gave me hope to see that, when he was interested or enjoying something, he was really able to focus, even if sometimes it was only for a few minutes. It was progress.

A few days later, Miss Loughran called me.

'Good news!' she exclaimed. 'Clover Woods has space for Ralph.'

They could only take him for three days a week for four hours each day but it was certainly better than nothing. On the other two days, he would continue to do two hours at his mainstream school.

'I think he's going to love it,' I replied.

Over the next week, I talked constantly about his new school.

'You get to play outside all day,' I told him. 'Even if it's raining. They give you special waterproof suits to wear so you can jump in the mud or make dens with sticks.'

'Sticks,' Ralph nodded.

When I talked to him about it, he seemed to listen, but I wasn't sure how much he was taking in. I even printed out some new pictures for his picture board for what was going to happen at school and to prepare him for the fact that he didn't have to wear a unform like he did at his old primary school.

One morning I took him to Clover Woods for a settling-in session. I'd talked about the school constantly but I could see that, even with me there, he was getting unsettled. The 'whooping' started as we pulled up into the car park and it took me a while to get him out of the car.

The staff were absolutely lovely and a woman called Stacey, who would be working with Ralph one-to-one at first, came out to the car park to talk to him. She looked young, probably in her twenties, and was full of energy and enthusiasm. Ralph stared at her, his blue eyes full of suspicion.

'We've made a campfire in the woods today, Ralph, and we're making pancakes,' she told him.

'Pancakes,' he nodded.

'Do you want to come and see?' Stacey asked him.

He turned around to look at me.

'Maggie will come too,' I nodded.

Slowly and very hesitantly, Ralph followed her through the woods to where five or six other children were gathered around a campfire. They were all different ages and they were whisking up some pancake batter in plastic bowls.

But Ralph's gaze was on the fire and I could see that he was transfixed.

'Hot,' he nodded.

'Yes, it's really hot,' Stacey told him. 'That's why we can't touch it and we have to stand back at a safe distance.'

'Fire,' he nodded.

We only stayed for an hour and Ralph seemed to enjoy making and eating his pancake.

'Did you like it at Clover Woods?' I asked him as we drove home in the car. 'Would you like to go to school there on some days?'

'Fire,' he nodded and I took that as a yes.

He started the following week and, amazingly, Ralph didn't make a fuss when I dropped him off on his first morning. He was exhausted when he came home but the staff said he had seemed to really enjoy it.

Long may it continue, I thought to myself.

One afternoon, Shelley had arranged to pop round and see me. I knew she must have something significant to discuss if she was coming in person rather than calling or messaging. I made sure that I mentioned it to Ralph several times.

When Shelley arrived, he was busy playing with his cars. She said hello to him but he didn't look up or engage with her.

'He seems very calm today,' she told me.

'We're slowly getting there,' I told her. 'Things have definitely improved. He's managing to use the toilet, although I still have to remind him and regularly take him, and he seems more settled generally. I think going to the new school has made a massive difference.'

I made us both a coffee and we sat at the kitchen table.

Shelley explained that she had reached out to the adoption team at the local authority where Ralph's half-sisters lived.

'They let the adopters know that the girls have a half-brother and they have come back to say they'd really like to meet him.'

While the girls, at eleven and nine, were old enough to understand that they had a half-sibling, I knew Ralph wasn't. Even if I did try to explain it to him, I don't think he would have understood what it meant.

'If they want to meet him then that's fine by me,' I said, 'but I'm not sure how he's going to react to them as he's had a lot of change in his life recently.'

'Their adoption worker has explained to them that you won't be able to answer any questions or give them any information about why Ralph came into the care system and what he's been through as that's confidential and they understand that,' Shelley told me. 'Although they live in a town three hours' drive from your house, they've suggested a country park that's only an hour away from here – they said they didn't mind the longer journey.'

Shelley also told me they'd suggested that they took the girls out of school for the day during the week when we met so it would be a lot quieter there.

'That's fine by me,' I said. 'It would be better for Ralph too – less chance of him feeling overwhelmed.'

Shelley told me the adoptive parents were called Chris and Lynn, and their adopted daughters were eleven-year-old Darcey and Teagan, nine.

'All they know about you is your first name and that Ralph is six,' she said.

She'd agreed with us all to meet up the following Tuesday.

'Do you think it would be possible to call them the night before just so we can arrange what time to meet and where?' I asked her.

'I'm sure Lynn won't mind me giving you her number,' replied Shelley.

I spent the next week telling Ralph all about it.

'On Tuesday we're going to meet Chris and Lynn at a park,' I told him. 'And their daughters Darcey and Teagan are coming too.'

I paused.

'And the special thing about Darcey and Teagan is that they're your sisters,' I said. 'They came out of your mummy's tummy just like you did.'

I looked at Ralph as I told him this information.

'Sisters,' he nodded.

'Yes, that's right,' I smiled. 'They're your sisters.'

He didn't say anything else.

I explained how we'd have a long drive in the car and I showed him pictures of a car park and swings and slides that I'd printed out and a picture of a café.

'We might have some lunch at the café,' I said.

'Sausages,' Ralph replied.

'Yes, they might have sausages there,' I nodded.

The day before we were due to meet, I called Lynn. I was intrigued about what she would be like and I was really pleased that she sounded so warm and friendly.

'The girls are so excited about meeting Ralph,' she told me.

'Ralph's obviously a lot younger than them and he's been through a lot recently,' I explained. 'I'm sure his social worker wouldn't mind me telling you this but he's also recently been diagnosed with autism so he might not react to the girls in the way that they're expecting.'

I went on to explain that he got anxious sometimes and his speech was limited.

'I completely understand,' replied Lynn. 'Teagan is autistic too. She sometimes struggles a lot in social situations and she'll probably be wearing her ear defenders when we meet up as she can find busy playgrounds overwhelming.'

We chatted for ten minutes and I felt really reassured.

Ralph thankfully had a good sleep the night before we were due to meet up. I was dreading the drive there but I brought lots of snacks and he had his felt cars clutched in both hands and he managed to stay calm. I'd arranged to meet Lynn by the entrance to the playground. As we walked towards it, my eyes scanned the crowd. I saw a woman with bobbed dark hair in a padded blue jacket and a pink scarf and jeans; I knew from the description she'd given me that it was her.

She saw me straight away too and gave us a wave.

'There's Lynn,' I told Ralph cheerfully.

I took his hand and walked over to her.

'Maggie?' she questioned.

'Yes,' I nodded. 'Lovely to meet you.'

'And this must be Ralph,' she smiled.

'Hi, Ralph,' she told him but he was busy staring at the swings.

'Chris is over there with the girls,' she said. 'Darcey's moaning that she's too old to go on a playground but Teagan's having a good time.'

She gestured over to a blond man sitting on a bench with an older girl. She had long hair the same colour as Ralph's and the same intense blue eyes.

Next to them was a younger girl sitting on the ground near the swings. She was picking up the wood chippings and sprinkling them through her fingers.

'That's Teagan,' smiled Lynn. 'Always doing her own thing.'

She was indeed wearing ear defenders, as Lynn had mentioned on the phone.

We went over to the girls and Lynn introduced us.

'This is Maggie, who is Ralph's foster carer,' she told them.

'Hi,' said Darcey, still looking fed up.

Teagan gave us a shy smile. 'Is that boy our brother?' she asked loudly.

'Yes, that's right, darling,' Lynn nodded. 'Remember how we talked about how you had the same tummy mummy?'

Teagan nodded and Ralph stared at her curiously.

'Thanks for agreeing to this,' Chris told me. 'It's just part of our girls' past and we felt it was important for them to have the opportunity to meet him.'

'I completely understand,' I nodded.

Chris had given Darcey some money to go and get an ice cream from the café and while we talked, I noticed Ralph had sat down on the ground close to Teagan. They didn't say anything to each other but Ralph was copying what Teagan was doing and was picking up the woodchips and throwing them.

'I think someone's made a friend,' smiled Lynn.

While the children seemed OK, we chatted.

'So I've been told that you're a nurse and Chris is a youth worker?' I asked Lynn.

'*Was* a youth worker,' she replied. 'Unfortunately he lost his job a few months ago.'

'Oh, I'm sorry to heart that,' I said.

'It has been hard but it's been nice having him around to help with the girls when I'm working shifts,' she said. 'Plus it's given us some thinking time and we realised that it was time for our lives to follow a new direction.'

She explained that they'd spent the past few months going through the process to be assessed as foster carers.

'It's something we've wanted to do for a while,' she told me. 'We couldn't have children of our own and we felt so lucky getting the girls. I know it sounds cheesy but we wanted to give something back.'

'Not at all,' I nodded. 'I've been doing this job for over twenty years and I completely understand what you mean.'

We talked about the assessment process and where they were at.

'We were approved at panel about a month ago but we haven't been matched with a child yet,' she said.

She paused.

'So it seemed a bit like fate when our adoption worker got in touch and told us about Ralph.'

I hadn't been expecting this.

Suddenly I could see where all this was going and I wasn't sure if I was prepared for it.

NINETEEN

All Change

In my heart I knew what was coming. However, I didn't get the call until a couple of days later.

'How did it go with Chris and Lynn the other day?' Shelley asked me.

'It went well,' I told her. 'They seem like a really lovely family.'

'And how did Ralph cope with it all?'

'It's hard to tell,' I shrugged. 'As always, you're never sure how much he understands.'

I explained that he seemed to have made an instant connection with Teagan.

'He sat near Teagan for ages and copied what she was doing, which was really sweet,' I said.

'Aah, that's lovely,' Shelley replied.

Then she paused.

'I'm ringing because there's something I want to run by you,' she said.

She explained how she'd had a call from Chris and Lynn's adoption worker.

'I'm not sure how to say this, Maggie,' she told me. 'But they've said they're interested in fostering Ralph long-term.'

'I suspected that,' I replied. 'As soon as Lynn mentioned they'd been approved as foster carers a few weeks ago, I wondered if that's why they wanted to meet him.'

'The timing couldn't be more convenient in a way,' replied Shelley.

'Their adoption worker is going to put me in touch with Chris and Lynn's supervising social worker,' she added. 'But before I chatted to them, I wanted to get your thoughts as obviously you've had Ralph for the past few months and I don't want to step on your toes. Is having him long-term something that you've considered?' Shelley asked. 'How would you feel about them potentially fostering him?'

I thought about it for a moment.

'I'm not going to lie to you,' I sighed. 'Having Ralph has been a real challenge and there have been times that I've been utterly exhausted and felt like I couldn't do it anymore. But I've grown so, so fond of him and I feel really protective towards him.'

I paused.

'I would always be willing to foster him for the long-term but I want the best for him and if the option of being with his half-sisters is there, I can't let myself stand in the way of that.'

As adopted children grew up, I knew they were often left wondering about their birth parents and they missed having that biological connection. At least this way, Ralph would have his sisters, particularly as none of them had contact with either of their birth parents. As they got older, it was going to be important for them to have that shared family history and I knew Social Services always preferred to place children with family members if possible.

'Thank you, Maggie,' Shelley told me. 'I know you're close to Ralph and this must be hard for you but we both know how important a biological connection can be for children in the care system.'

The next step was for Shelley to contact Chris and Lynn's supervising social worker and have a chat.

'My only worry is that they're going to struggle to cope with Ralph's behaviour,' I told her. 'What if he leaves here to be with them and they realise that they can't manage him?'

I reminded her how he'd already been rejected by two carers before coming to me.

'We'll have to talk to them very honestly about that,' agreed Shelley. 'I'll have a full and frank conversation with their supervising social worker and fill them in on Ralph's background and why he came into the care system and the ongoing challenges of his behaviour.'

I remembered how he had been when he'd first come to live at my house and how his behaviour had been improving over the past few weeks.

'I've been working so hard to keep everything consistent and stable for him and I just worry that he will struggle to cope with more change,' I said. 'And there are his additional needs to manage.'

'Their adoption worker did say Chris and Lynn were open to fostering children with disabilities,' she told me. 'And, as we know, their youngest daughter is autistic.'

'But I think it's a bit different trying to manage two children with additional needs,' I said.

Shelley said she would have these conversations with all concerned and report back.

It was four days before she got in touch with me again.

'You were right, Maggie,' said Shelley. 'They seem like a lovely couple. I really liked them.'

'Were they put off by Ralph's background?' I asked.

'They didn't seem to be,' she said. 'Lynn got very emotional when she heard what he'd been through. Sadly, it's a similar story to the girls. They weren't physically hurt by Renae but they both suffered appalling neglect as well.'

She explained that the couple were very conscious of upsetting me.

'Don't worry, I'll have a chat to them when I see them,' I told her.

Unlike adoption, settling a child in with a new foster carer was a fairly quick process that was normally done in a matter of days. But, after everything Ralph had been through, Shelley was in agreement that it needed to happen more slowly, over a couple of weeks.

'But what about school?' I asked. 'Ralph is doing really well at Clover Woods. I don't think he would cope having to transition back to a mainstream school.'

'I've spoken at length to Chris and Lynn about it and they are hopeful there will be a place for him at Teagan's school.'

Shelley explained that, while it wasn't a forest setting like Clover Woods, it was a special school for children with autism and other additional needs.

'Apparently Teagan is really happy there,' Shelley told me. 'And if there isn't a place straight away, Chris and Lynn have said they will home-school Ralph.'

That alleviated my worries a little bit.

The first step was Chris and Lynn getting to know Ralph better on their own without the girls being there.

Shelley had organised for them to drive up to my house one day when the girls were at school and spend a couple of hours with Ralph and I.

I kept him off school that morning.

'You're not going to school today because Chris and Lynn are coming to visit you,' I told him.

He stared at me blankly.

'Remember we met them at the country park?' I said. 'Darcey and Teagan's mummy and daddy.'

'Teagan,' nodded Ralph.

'That's right,' I told him. 'You liked Teagan, didn't you?'

When they arrived, Ralph was playing cars in the kitchen so I went to the front door to let them in. I could tell that they were nervous.

'Come on in,' I smiled. 'You've had a long drive. Ralph's engrossed in his cars at the moment.'

'Thanks so much, Maggie,' said Chris.

Lynn hung back awkwardly and I could tell there was something she wanted to say to me.

'I don't want you to think we were hiding anything from you,' she told me. 'When we met you the other week, we didn't really know what we were doing. We wanted to meet Ralph and see the kind of child he was and then take it from there. I just feel really guilty and I don't want you to feel like we're swooping in and taking Ralph from you.'

'Not at all,' I replied.

'When the adoption worker told us about Ralph and it was

a few weeks after we'd been accepted as foster carers, it just felt like it was meant to be somehow,' smiled Lynn.

'I think it was,' I told her. 'I would never stand in the way of Ralph being able to be with his sisters. That bond, that link to his past, will be so important to him as he grows up,' I added. 'And for your girls too.'

'Thank you for understanding,' said Chris.

We all headed to the kitchen where Ralph was lying on the floor with his cars.

'Ralph, Chris and Lynn are here,' I told him.

He looked up at them expectantly but he didn't say a word and his gaze quickly went back to his vehicles.

'Give him time,' I told them.

'Don't worry,' Lynn told me. 'We're prepared for that.'

I knew it was going to be baby steps with Ralph.

We chatted for a while and had a cup of tea. At one point, Chris went to sit on the floor near Ralph and talked to him about his cars. Ralph didn't say anything to him. He didn't show any reaction.

'Just a word of warning, he can get very protective about his cars,' I told him.

'Teagan's the same but with her it's her cuddly toys,' replied Lynn. 'She won't let anyone touch them.'

Ralph suddenly looked up.

'Teagan,' he repeated.

'That's right,' smiled Lynn. 'Do you remember Teagan from the park?'

He nodded.

'He really seems to have taken a liking to Teagan,' I said to them.

Before they left, we agreed that the following weekend I would bring Ralph to their house and we'd stay for a couple of hours.

'It's such a long drive for you,' said Chris.

'I think it's really important that he sees the house and starts to get used to being there,' I told them.

And, I thought at first, it would be good for Ralph to have me there with him.

Shelley rang me that afternoon to see how their visit had gone.

'It went well,' I told her. 'Ralph didn't particularly engage with them but I wasn't expecting him to. He didn't show any negative reaction to them either, though, which is good.'

Shelley said she'd also got something else that she needed to tell me.

'Renae appeared in court today,' she told me.

It was a shock.

'None of us realised it was happening today,' she added. 'DC Mitchell just gave me a call to update me.'

She'd pleaded guilty to neglect and child abduction and would be sentenced in a few months. The CPS were sure she was going to get a custodial sentence.

'Wow,' I sighed. 'She admitted it.'

'Yep,' nodded Shelley. 'At least she did the right thing in the end.'

It was a relief. There was always the risk that Ralph would have had to be interviewed by the police if there was going to be a trial – at least she'd spared him from that.

It was one last thing that she could do for her son.

On Saturday, we drove over to Chris and Lynn's house. I was nervous about the long journey but we stopped two or three times and Ralph had his felt cars and lots of snacks. He was very calm until we pulled up outside their house – a 1930's semi on a quiet cul-de-sac.

He started whooping and bucking in his car seat.

'Ralph, it's OK,' I soothed. 'This is Chris and Lynn's house and you're going to see Darcey and Teagan.'

'Teagan,' he nodded.

'That's right,' I said.

He clung to my side for most of the hour we were there but Chris and Lynn made such an effort. They'd made pancakes, which Ralph wolfed down, and they gave us a tour of the house, showing us the box room that was next to their bedroom at the front.

'We're hoping this is going to be Ralph's room,' Lynn said.

'Wow, Ralph,' I said. 'Wouldn't that be lovely, to come and sleep at Chris and Lynn's house?'

Ralph stared back at me with a blank look on his face.

'We can paint the walls in your favourite colour,' Chris told him.

'Tell Chris, what's your favourite colour, Ralph?' I asked him.

'Blue,' he said straight away. 'I like blue. And sausages.'

We all laughed.

'I don't think we're going to have sausages in your bedroom but you can definitely have them for breakfast,' smiled Lynn.

Ralph was still fascinated by Teagan and his gaze followed her around the room. He stared as she stroked the family's pet tabby cat.

'That's Fluffy,' Lynn told him. 'She sleeps on Teagan's bed every night.'

Teagan nodded.

'She likes me the best,' she said proudly.

I could see Ralph watching everything and everyone and taking it all in.

The next step was a few days later – Chris and Lynn were coming to collect Ralph and take him to their house to stay overnight. I wanted him to be as prepared as possible so I'd asked them to take lots of photos of themselves and their house and garden and send them to me. I printed them all out and put them in clear plastic envelopes and stuck them around the house. I knew Ralph seemed to understand things more when they were presented to him visually and I constantly talked about them.

'You're going to Chris and Lynn's house tomorrow,' I told him, pointing to a photo of it. 'And this is their kitchen, where you'll have lunch and dinner and breakfast the next morning.

'And this is Ralph's room,' I told him, pointing to another picture. 'Instead of sleeping at Maggie's house, you're going to sleep at Chris and Lynn's house.'

He didn't say a word.

Later that afternoon, I was packing a bag for him to take with him the following day.

'You'll need your pyjamas when you sleep at Chris and Lynn's house,' I told him, folding them up and putting them into the bag.

'No sleep at Maggie's house,' said Ralph firmly.

I went and got the picture board.

'No – remember you're going to sleep at Chris and Lynn's house. Which is Chris and Lynn's house?'

He pointed at the picture on the board.

'That's right,' I said.

'Then you're going to sleep in Ralph's new room. Where's Ralph's room?'

He pointed to the photo of his bedroom.

'Sleep at Chris and Lynn's,' he said.

'That's right,' I nodded. 'Tomorrow you're going to sleep at Chris and Lynn's. And you'll see Darcey and Teagan.'

Ralph looked up at me and slowly the corners of his mouth crinkled and he broke out into a little smile.

'See Teagan,' he grinned and my heart swelled. Ralph wasn't a child who laughed or smiled much. To see him smile truly felt like progress and it was so lovely to see.

And for the rest of the afternoon, he repeated to himself: 'See Teagan. See Teagan.'

I was under no illusions that it was going to be easy but I could see that it was starting to sink in for him.

TWENTY

Letting Go

Up until now, I hadn't said anything to Amena about Ralph leaving in case it didn't happen. But now, it felt like the time had come to say something.

'Why are there photos of these people all over the house?' she asked. 'Who are they?'

'I need to tell you something,' I said. 'That is Chris and Lynn, and we think Ralph's going to go and live with them and his half-sisters.'

I explained what had happened and how they'd got in touch with Social Services.

'I couldn't tell you for confidentiality reasons before now, but Ralph's met them a few times and it looks like they're going to be fostering him long-term.'

'Oh,' she said, looking surprised. 'That's a bit sad. I know he can be really annoying sometimes but I'll miss him.'

'Me too,' I replied, giving her hand a squeeze. 'But it's happy news really. It's lovely for Ralph that he gets to go and live with his sisters. That's a good thing.'

I didn't know whether I was trying to convince Amena or myself. Yes, it was a good thing but it didn't stop the heavy sense of sadness I felt when I dropped Ralph off at Chris and Lynn's house the next day and saw his confused little face at the window as I drove away.

It all suddenly felt very real.

'I've said goodbye to so many children over the years but I can honestly say that I never get used to it,' I told Vicky on the phone that night. 'He's only there for one night and I can't stop worrying about how he's getting on.'

'That's normal,' she sighed. 'Yes, you're a foster carer but also you're a person with a big heart and feelings. It's normal to get attached.'

'I just want it to go well for Ralph,' I said. 'He's been through so much.'

'It will,' Vicky reassured me.

It was good to chat to her as, with everything going on with Ralph, we hadn't had chance to talk for a few weeks.

'Have you had any more thoughts about your fostering?' I asked her.

The line went quiet.

'I've been doing a lot of soul-searching and I think I'm going to carry on,' she said. 'At least for a little while longer.'

'Oh, I'm so pleased,' I told her. 'I can't imagine you not being a foster carer.'

'I don't think I'm quite ready to have a placement just yet but maybe in a few weeks,' she said.

I was sure she had made the right decision and welcoming another child or children into her home would help heal her broken heart. I hoped so anyway.

*

The following day, Chris and Lynn were going to drop Ralph back and stay for tea. I was keen to know how his overnight stay had gone. I'd told them to call me if they were having any problems but I hadn't heard anything.

When they arrived, I could immediately tell that something wasn't right. They all looked exhausted and they were quiet and subdued over dinner. Ralph kept yawning and I could see he was tired too.

'How did it go?' I asked when the girls and Ralph went to watch some TV while we cleared up.

Chris and Lynn looked at each other.

'It was a really hard night,' sighed Lynn, looking close to tears. 'Ralph was very unsettled.'

'To be honest, I'm not surprised,' I told them. 'I think Ralph will be very up and down at first and it's going to take him time to adjust.'

They described how he had hardly slept, he'd trashed the bedroom and soiled the floor several times.

'It had all been freshly painted as well and we'd put new carpet down,' nodded Lynn.

They looked broken and I had a sick feeling in my stomach.

'I hope you don't mind me asking you this,' I said, 'but are you having second thoughts about taking him on?'

It was my biggest fear but I would rather them say it now than get further down the line and have to let Ralph down.

'No,' said Chris. 'It was just a lot.'

'I think reality hit home last night and we realised it's going to take time for Ralph to settle,' added Lynn.

'I've struggled with Ralph so much at times,' I nodded. 'There were points when I wondered if I was going to be able to cope.'

'I can promise you we're going into this with our eyes open,' said Chris.

However, I still had doubts and I spoke to Shelley about it.

'I can't bear for Ralph to be rejected again,' I said. 'The thought of it breaks my heart.'

'I will say they do seem committed,' Shelley said. 'I know Chris is going to be at home full-time and their local authority is going to offer them extra support if they need it.'

'If they do find it too much and they feel they can't cope, I would be willing to take Ralph back,' I told her.

I would always be there for him.

'Thanks, Maggie,' Shelley replied. 'That means a lot.'

Ralph was due to have one more overnight stay with Chris and Lynn before he moved there permanently. This time they were coming to pick him up and start to take a few boxes of his stuff over with them.

Thankfully this time things went a lot more smoothly. When they dropped him back, everyone was smiling – even Ralph.

'How was it?' I asked.

'He still took a while to settle but it was so much better than the last time,' Lynn told me.

They'd encouraged him to help them unpack some of his things and put them in his new bedroom.

I was so relieved things had gone well.

'See you in a couple of days,' said Lynn excitedly.

They were coming on Saturday to collect Ralph and take him back to their house for good.

In Ralph's case, I knew there was no need for a big goodbye. The best thing I could do was continue to keep everything low key and consistent for him. Somehow, I also had to try to help him to understand that he wasn't coming back to my house and that he was going to live at Chris and Lynn's house permanently.

I continually showed him and talked about the photographs and pointed out his bedroom to him and photos of Chris and Lynn and the girls. On his final night, I made all three of us sausages and mash for dinner – Ralph's favourite.

'Tomorrow's going to be a really exciting day, Ralph,' I told him. 'You're going to sleep at Maggie's house tonight and then tomorrow you're going to live at Chris and Lynn's house with Teagan and Darcey.'

'Live Teagan's house,' he nodded.

'That's right,' I smiled. 'And you're going to sleep in your blue bedroom and it's going to be your home. Maggie and Amena will miss you but—'

'Live Teagan's house,' he repeated.

'It's going to be so cool that you'll be with your sisters, Ralph,' Amena told him.

'Live Teagan's house,' he said again.

I hoped the message had finally sunk in.

We had moved most of Ralph's stuff over to their house already. All that was left were his precious car collection and a change of clothes and a few toiletries. The following morning, he watched me pack his last few things into a bag before Chris and Lynn arrived.

'Bye-bye, Maggie's bedroom,' I said, waving as we went downstairs.

When Chris and Lynn arrived, I could see how excited they were.

'It feels like Christmas Day but I'm nervous too,' smiled Lynn.

She explained the girls were at home with Chris's mum.

'They're so excited,' she added. 'They've baked a cake and made a sign saying: "Welcome Home Ralph".'

'That's lovely,' I said.

As Ralph watched Chris load his bag into the boot of their car, I knew there was no putting off the inevitable now.

Ralph had never been a child who was overly keen on physical contact and he didn't like hugs, so I ruffled his hair and gently stroked his cheek.

'Bye-bye, Ralph,' I said. 'I'm going to miss you but I know you're going to be really happy at Teagan's house.'

'Live Teagan's house,' he replied.

'That's right,' I nodded.

Amena and I walked him down to the car and I handed him his felt cars to hold during the journey.

'Maggie's cars,' said Ralph.

'No, they're yours – you can take them with you in Chris and Lynn's car,' I told him.

I helped strap him into his car seat and then closed the door. I blew him a kiss through the window.

Chris and Lynn gave me a hug.

'Thank you so, so much,' said Lynn, who was a bit teary. 'I promise you we'll look after him.'

'I know you will,' I told her.

Then we watched them drive off into the distance.

'Bye-bye, Ralph!' shouted Amena, but he looked completely disinterested as he examined his cars.

I knew I needed to hold it together for Amena's sake so I swallowed the lump in my throat.

We walked up the path and I closed the front door.

'Let's go and have a cup of tea,' I told her. 'We could even go to the cinema tonight if you wanted?'

Since we'd had Ralph, we hadn't been able to do anything in the evenings.

Suddenly, much to my surprise, Amena burst into tears.

'Oh, lovey,' I sighed, putting my arms around her. 'What's the matter?'

'Do you think Ralph's going to be OK?' she sobbed. 'I feel really bad for him.'

'I think he's going to be absolutely fine,' I told her. 'He's with his sisters and Chris and Lynn are really lovely.'

'I just feel so sad,' she told me.

I gave her a squeeze.

'That's because you're a kind person with a big heart,' I said. 'I feel sad too but it's a good thing for Ralph.'

Amena never failed to impress me with her strength of her compassion – she really was a wonderful girl and I wasn't looking forward to the time when she too would move on. I forced myself to be upbeat for the rest of the evening as I wanted to reassure her that Ralph going to live with Chris and Lynn was the right thing for him.

It was only when I knew she was in bed later that night that I allowed myself to sit on the sofa and have a good cry. All my sadness and worry was able to come out now that I was alone with my thoughts.

A few minutes later, my phone beeped.

It was a picture of Ralph, curled up in bed with a car

clutched in each hand and Fluffy the cat fast asleep at his feet.

Think Fluffy has a new friend! Lynn had written. *So far, so good. Thank you for everything x*

I had to tell myself that Ralph was going to be OK. It really was the best-case scenario for him to be able to grow up with his half-sisters. He'd been through so much at the hands of his parents but with love, patience and understanding from his new family, I knew that at last he was going to have the happy, settled life that he deserved.

The phone call came a couple of months later.

'Lynn!' I said. 'It's so nice to hear from you. How are things?'

She explained that they'd just had a phone call from Shelley.

'I felt like I should let you know,' she said. 'Renae was sentenced today. The judge gave her three years in prison.'

My gut reaction was that it didn't seem enough for everything Ralph had been through.

'Have you said anything to Ralph?' I asked her.

'We've tried,' said Lynn. 'But I don't think he understood. All we can do is be honest with him and hope that, as he gets older, he starts to take it in.'

'How's he doing?' I asked.

I'd encouraged her to message me and we'd been in touch every few days at first but slowly the contact had dwindled off. We had all agreed that Ralph seeing me very soon after moving might unsettle him and also, of course, the family lived three hours away.

'It has been utterly exhausting,' she laughed. 'I don't know how you managed him on your own. Both me and Chris are like zombies.'

'It sounds like he's putting you through your paces,' I said light-heartedly.

'He certainly is,' she said. 'But we're staying consistent and I honestly do think we've turned a corner.

'He's settling in at his new school and he and Teagan have formed a lovely bond. And he adores Fluffy.'

'Bless him,' I smiled.

Lynn explained how Ralph's behaviour had started to calm down and he was managing to use the toilet now. She described how the paediatrician had recently prescribed him a medication that was helping him fall asleep faster and stay asleep for longer.

'It took a few days but thankfully he's not waking up at silly-o'clock anymore or getting up and down in the night,' she sighed. 'It's made such a difference to all of us being able to get some proper sleep.'

'I bet,' I replied. 'I know what that feels like when you're just not getting any rest. You can't think straight.'

'And it means Ralph's behaviour is a bit more settled in the day and he can concentrate at school,' Lynn added.

She mentioned that he had also started speech and language sessions at school.

'It's a slow process,' sighed Lynn. 'But he's definitely saying more words and short sentences now, and Shelley has put him on a waiting list to get some play therapy.'

'That's wonderful,' I smiled. 'It will make such a difference with him being able to communicate and to express how he's feeling a bit more.'

We all knew that with Ralph, nothing was going to be instant but it all sounded like steps in the right direction.

'It makes me so happy to hear how well he's doing,' I told her. 'I think about him often.'

'And he does you,' Lynn replied. 'He'll often mention you and say "Sleep at Maggie's house", and me and Chris say, "That's right, you did sleep at Maggie's house, didn't you?". And we talk about Amena, and how we met up for the first time at the country park that day.'

It comforted me, as well as made me a bit teary, to know that somewhere, deep down, Ralph remembered me and the time he'd spent in my care. I knew that wouldn't last though and that was OK. I wanted him to let go so he could fully move on in his new life with Chris and Lynn and his half-sisters.

'There's one thing I want you to know, Maggie,' Lynn told me. 'Whatever happens, whatever the future may hold, we're not going to give up on Ralph.

'As he gets older, I know there will be issues and problems but we'll work through them together. We're in this for the long haul.'

'That's wonderful,' I said.

In my heart, I was sure that Ralph had found his forever family. All little ones deserve that but sadly it didn't happen for everyone.

When deeply troubled children walked through my door, I couldn't change what they had been through. All I could do was help them to move on and make sure their future was much brighter. For Ralph, with Chris, Lynn and his sisters by his side, I was sure that it was.

Acknowledgements

Thank you to my children, Tess, Pete and Sam, who are such a big part of my fostering today. However, I had not met you when Amena and Ralph came into my home. To my wide circle of fostering friends – you know who you are! Your support and your laughter are valued. To my friend Andrew B for your continued encouragement and care. Thanks also to Heather Bishop, who spent many hours listening and enabled this story to be told, my literary agent Rowan Lawton and to Anna Valentine, Vicky Eribo and Beth Eynon at Seven Dials for giving me the opportunity to share these stories.

Maggie Hartley has fostered more than 300 children while being a foster carer for over twenty years. Taking on the children other carers often can't cope with, Maggie helps children that are deemed 'unadoptable' because of their behaviour or the extreme trauma that they've been through.

She's looked after refugees, supported children through sexual abuse and violence court cases, cared for teenagers on remand and taught young mums how to parent their newborn babies.

You can find her on Facebook at MaggieHartleyAuthor, where she would love to hear from you.

'Mummy! Where did you go? Please come back, Mummy.'

When police are called to a local supermarket late one evening, they find an angry shopkeeper and a silent young woman. It's the third time 24-year-old Zoe has been caught stealing in the past few days. Eyes filled with panic, Zoe has been hiding bread, milk, Calpol and nappies under her coat. As police officers break down the door of Zoe's flat they find seven-year-old Coco and three-year-old Lola, home alone, huddled on the floor in a freezing cold bedroom, crying out for their mummy.

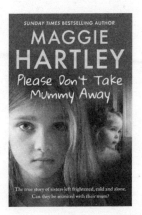

When Social Services are called in, the girls are taken into care and are soon tucked up safely in bed at Maggie's house. It looks like a simple case of neglect, but things aren't always what they seem and, with Maggie's help, can Zoe convince Social Services that love is enough to be a good mum?

Read on for an extract from *Please Don't Take Mummy Away*, available now in paperback, eBook and audio.

The call came through on the radio of the police car just as they were taking the first bite of the sandwiches they'd bought at the supermarket. PC Caroline Davidson looked wearily at her shift partner, PC Robbie Hunt.

'Shoplifter at a corner shop,' he sighed. 'Hardly the crime of the century.'

Normally a shoplifter would be way down on their list of callouts but, for once in as long as Caroline could remember, it had been a quiet night shift so far.

'We'd better go,' she told him. 'It's only two minutes down the road.'

'Really?' he said and she nodded.

'OK then,' he sighed, turning the engine on. 'You can be the one who gives the teenager the lecture while they spit and swear at you.'

The shop, a little off-licence and mini-market, was a one-minute drive from where they were parked. To be honest, they probably could have walked there quicker.

The door of the shop beeped loudly as they pushed it open. There was a disgruntled-looking elderly man sitting behind the counter on a stool.

'About time,' he sighed. 'She's in the stockroom. This ain't the first time she's done it. She's in here every few days, thinks she can just take what she wants. I knew she was up to something, only this time the shop was quiet so I spotted her on the cameras. It'll be on CCTV so there's proof. I want her done for this.'

Her, thought Caroline.

For some reason, she'd assumed it would be a teenaged boy.

'Probably a druggie,' the shopkeeper sighed. 'She's got that look about her. Skinny as a rake with weird eyes that stare right through you.'

He turned the sign to 'Closed', locked the shop door and led them through to the back.

'Here she is,' he told them.

Cowering in the corner of the stockroom was a young woman. Caroline had been expecting a teenager and although she was young, the lines etched on the woman's face suggested that she was older.

She looked up at them with fearful green eyes.

'I told you I'd call the police on you,' the shopkeeper raged. 'You've been stealing from me for months, making a mockery of my livelihood. Well you're gonna pay for it big time now.'

The woman was silent but Caroline could see that she was shaking with fear.

'Go on then,' he hissed. 'What you got to say for yourself?'

'I'm sorry,' she said in a voice so quiet, it was almost a whisper.

'She's admitting it,' the shopkeeper nodded triumphantly.

'Please just let me go,' begged the young woman. 'I promise I won't do it again. I'll pay you back for it all. Just tell me how much I owe you and I'll find a way.'

The shopkeeper laughed then he turned to Caroline and Robbie.

'I want to press charges,' he said. 'I've got the CCTV footage I can give you.'

'OK,' said Robbie. 'Let's get you down to the station.'

The woman gasped and put her head in her hands.

'Please,' she said. 'I'm begging you. Don't make me come down to the station. I can come another time but not now.'

'I'm afraid you can't pick and choose when we interview you,' Robbie told her. 'We'll need to take you down to the station to get a few details and ask you some questions.'

The woman was in floods of tears.

'Please don't do this,' she sobbed. 'I'm begging you.'

There was something about this frail young woman that made Caroline think they were being overzealous.

'Can I have a quick word?' she asked her colleague.

She and Robbie stepped outside the stockroom.

'Do we really have to make an example out of her like this?' she said in a low voice. 'It's just shoplifting. She looks desperate.'

'You heard the man,' he told her. 'He's got CCTV proof that she's broken the law. We can't just ignore it. Besides, if we take her to the station and give her a scare, it might stop her doing it again. Might give her another way to support her habit.'

Yes, she was thin and her face was so hollow you could see her cheekbones, but there was something about the young woman's appearance that told Caroline she wasn't on drugs.

'I just think she's been taught enough of a lesson,' she shrugged.

But there was no talking her colleague round.

The shopkeeper came out to join them.

'Are you gonna cuff her then?' he nodded. 'Send out a message to other scumbags who think it's OK to rip me off on a daily basis?'

'I don't think there's any need for that,' Robbie told him.

'Just one quick question,' Caroline asked him. 'What did she steal?'

He walked over to the till.

'This lot,' he said, putting an array of items on the counter. 'I reckon I caught her before she could get to the booze.'

Caroline looked at the items on the counter – a loaf of white bread, a carton of milk, some jam and crisps. But it was the final items that concerned her the most – two bottles of Calpol and a packet of pull-ups in a toddler size. Her heart sank.

'Let me have another word with her,' she said.

She went back into the stockroom where the young woman was sitting on a stool crying. Caroline perched down next to her.

'What's your name, darling?' she asked her.

'Zoe,' she whimpered.

'I saw the pull-ups that you stole, Zoe,' she told her. 'Do you have a child at home? Is that why you don't want to go down to the station with us?'

The woman didn't say a word, she just buried her head in her hands and sobbed.

'Please don't make me go to the station,' she said. 'I'm begging you. I need to go home.'

'Is your child home alone?' Caroline asked.

The woman sobbed even louder.

'Just let me go home. I promise I'll come to the station tomorrow.'

She looked up at her with desperate eyes.

Robbie came back in.

'Right then,' he said. 'Let's go.'

'Please don't do this,' sobbed the woman.

Caroline pulled her colleague to one side.

'Before we go anywhere, I think we need to call Social Services,' she said. 'It's an emergency.'